A MUST-HAVE **SKILLSET** FOR THE **FUTURE**

UNBOXING CREATIVITY

RID Framework to Survive and Thrive in Disruptive Times

A MUST-HAVE **SKILLSET** FOR THE **FUTURE**

UNBOXING CREATIVITY

RID Framework to Survive and Thrive in Disruptive Times

VIRUPAKSHAPPA

Worldwide Publishing by
Pendown Press

PENDOWN PRESS

An ISO 9001 & ISO 14001 Certified Co.,

Regd. Office: 2525/193, 1st Floor, Onkar Nagar-A,

Tri Nagar, Delhi-110035

Ph.: 09350849407, 09312235086

E-mail: info@pendownpress.com

Branch Office: 1A/2A, 20, Hari Sadan, Ansari Road,

Daryaganj, New Delhi-110002

Ph.: 011-45794768

Website: PendownPress.com

First Edition: 2023

ISBN: 978-93-5554-448-3

Layout and Cover Designed by Pendown Graphics Team

Illustration Designed by Pendown Press Illustration Team

Printed and Bound in India by Thomson Press India Ltd.

Dedication

To my beloved grandmother, late Smt. Thulasamma, my loving parents, Shri Kumarappa Hovale and Smt. Draupathi Bai, who have always been a vital source of inspiration and who gave me abundant love, provided a nurturing environment during my childhood years, enabling me to grow up as a confident person, striving towards my goals.

My heartfelt thanks to my Gurus, Trainers, Coaches and Mentors who supported me to learn and transform for the better, because of them I became stronger.

This book carries the strong support from my wife Suman and daughters Sanika and Kavyanjali, who constantly encouraged its progress and helped me follow through in delivering this book impressively.

My sincere gratitude to my sisters Shashirekha, Gayathri, Veena and Vasanthi for their best wishes, suggestions, and strong support on the completion of this book.

The very idea of a maiden book, every step from concept to final version, strengthening my will and commitment to focus and finally, a timely dose of spirituality were offered by Mr. Bhuwan Pant; without his guidance, writing this book would have been an impossible task for me, many thanks for the excellent guidance.

My heartfelt gratitude to a seasoned life coach, corporate trainer, and gentle person Mr. Sukhdeepak Malvai for his transformational support and impactful guidance.

I would also express my sincere thanks to all my childhood friends, college pals and colleagues, and seniors working around me, spread across multiple organizations for their strong motivation, and to the supreme Universe for the inspiration and support to publish this book.

Finally, my sincere thanks for all the editing help I received and the timely delivery of a well-crafted book by the publication team of M/s Pendown Press led by Mr. Dinesh Verma.

Contents

Introduction

My hearty congratulations on embarking on your new journey with this book in hand, creating your own compass for the hoped-for future. I am sure this will open up an abundance of possibilities, with the Universe supporting all of your good intentions.

How it started...!

It was in the midst of the COVID-19 pandemic during May 2020. Like most of us, I, too, was working from home with uncertainties around. Emotions were running high regarding the job, health, education for children, concerns about extended families and friends…. Oops…The list is pretty long!

I came across an interesting video clip (TED talk) on the well-known Titanic disaster story, but with a different perspective, relating to the business scenario and personal life.

The clip narrates in detail about various elements that led to the sinking of the Titanic ship, e.g., icebergs, binoculars, lifeboats, tools and a readiness to face emergencies, over-confidence in past successes in avoiding crashes, ignorance of external signals and competencies of the ship crew and captain.

The above story seeded in me even more interest in the topic of "Reinvention" and related topics that can positively impact our lives and sustain businesses, even thriving during challenges. Nevertheless, Reinvention is not just in business but in personal life too, to progress in an ever-changing environment despite being faced with various icebergs that we encounter on the journey of life.

In this publication, sincere efforts have been made to share impactful tools and approaches to business to live and thrive in a constantly evolving VUCA (Volatile, Uncertain, Complex, and Ambiguous) world.

With more than a decade of exposure to Strategic Planning and Execution in Industry, having seen the transformation and sinking of a few well-established enterprises; I was motivated to further hone my knowledge on related topics by going through formal learning on Design Thinking, Innovation, and also programs on Reinvention.

With this experience, I found really encouraging developments on various business aspects in product positioning, processes, and business expansion efforts to prepare oneself to survive the future while growing today.

Individuals keen on driving their functions, organizations, and themselves to not just survive today but thrive for tomorrow must initiate the necessary actions.

Enterprises fearing the unknown or lesser-known changes find it easy to navigate through elements of how to handle and absorb the weak signals of imminent changes, creating a

mindset and culture to respond appropriately within functions and across organizational levels.

Not being able to see, prepare and respond to a fast-changing business environment may prove to be a death knell for enterprises. Well-crafted change management by planned reinvention would prove extremely beneficial to keep businesses growing and thriving.

One of the most basic definitions of Reinvention is a way of running an enterprise where an organization demonstrates its capability by anticipating change, designing change, and successfully implementing those "change" aspects while retaining its core and carrying key success factors relevant to the future.

Lastly, you may wonder what about the topics of "Creativity", "Design Thinking", and "Innovation"; However, I am glad to clarify that all these elements are closely connected to each other and, as part of grand contours, complement each other. Ofcourse, Creativity is not just limited to arts, music or theatre, and paintings but in and around our businesses too.

My call to action is to pick every small element in your business you feel has the potential to threaten and also grow further. Then have a planned intervention by way of "Reinvention" using a host of tools, specifically the RID formula you find in this book.

Wishing you success in your "Creative" journey, leveraging the RID (Reinvention-Innovation-Design Thinking) formula to craft your hoped for future.

PART 1

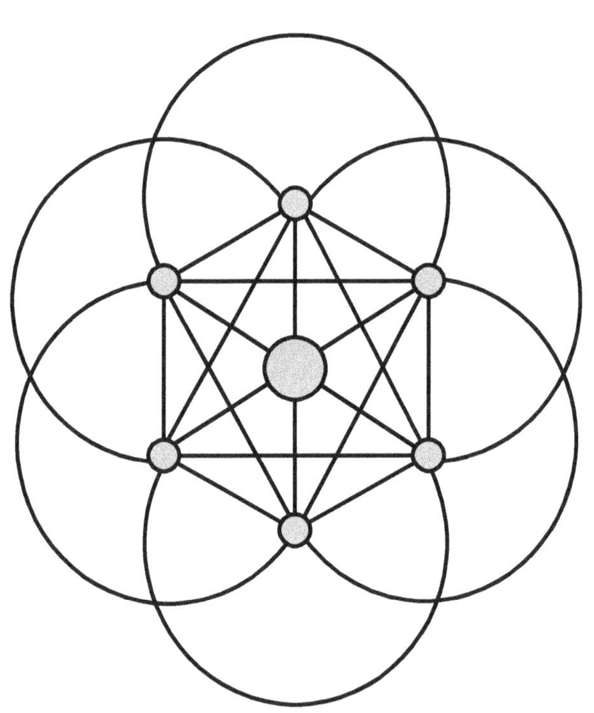

Unboxing The System – Jump Start With Creativity

"Creativity is inventing, experimenting, growing, taking risks, breaking the rules, making mistakes, and having fun."

~Mary Lou Cook, Peace Activist

A long due visit to my hometown fortunately also gave me an opportunity to meet my close friend at her residence in the same city. As I made myself comfortable on the plush sofa, one object that caught my attention in her tastefully decorated drawing room was an exquisite centerpiece, a glass topped table mounted on a beautiful brass urn. It was such a unique design, something I had not seen before, giving a very classic, chic look to the room.

On asking, she said that this huge, metallic vase lying in her parent's home had been with them for years, belonging to her grandparents, and now her parents didn't know what to do with it.

They were contemplating discarding it, though being a part of their heritage, they didn't wish to do so; obviously, there were sentiments attached! She applied her creative brilliance and got this antique vase converted into nothing less than a work of art – a centre table for her living room.

An experiment with her innate sense of home décor was such a success. The entire process, from finding an experienced woodworker who could do the task to perfection, designing it, getting the metal piece polished, selecting the finest glass, to the final work, was completed with such mastery!!

A fine wood and glass cupboard from her ancestral home got a similar makeover, making the space so aesthetically pleasing! Fulfilling the twin purpose of not just preserving the family legacy but giving a classic look to her house as well, in addition to the utility. Nobody could ever guess that these were decades-old furniture.

Isn't this creativity par excellence?

I truly marvel at her knack for finding the extraordinariness in simple things. A dash of imagination along with expanding our perception/limitations and lo and behold, a worthwhile innovative idea is born!

Chapter I

Why Creativity is Important – The 3C Approach to Start the Journey

A Fascinating Take On Creativity & How It Can Turbo-Charge Your Business

The secret of change is to focus all of your energy not on fighting the old but building on the new - Socrates (470-399 BC), Philosopher.

Won't you agree? All cultures are inherently predisposed to change, yet we resist transformation.

It's crucial to understand that a society has psychological changes, alterations in our natural environment, evolving needs, and aspirations. So, we need to continuously look for new tools, fresh energy sources, and advanced technology to meet the growing demands of our society.

How do you think we look for new tools?

Through Creativity!

'Creativity' is the essential attitude required for an effective change. It is creativity that leads to the evolution of new products and services.

Do you remember reading about the Indus Valley Civilisation, also known as Harappan Civilisation, that existed between 3300 to 1300 BCE?

The history of this civilisation is mysterious. But there are enough sources to reveal that its people displayed high levels of creativity. There exist a plethora of inventions and endeavours indicating refined artistic sensibilities and vivid imagination of people during that era. Let's discuss these creative and technological achievements below!

- **The invention of the step-well (a bathing pool having stairs leading towards the water):** Also known as the world's first known urban sanitation system, a step-well is one of the best inventions of that time.

  Harappans also created the "Great Bath" in MohenjoDaro, seen today as the size of a modest municipal swimming pool. These developments may look ordinary to us at this moment. But conceptualising a step well or public bath during 3300 to 1300 BC was a result of some extraordinarily creative minds.

- **Well-Structured Living and Housing Areas:** These were grid-planned cities in South Asia; each block was subdivided by a small lane.

- **Intricate Jewellery:** Indus people made jewellery from gold and agate. Archaeologists also found numerous

remains of artefacts and toys for children. Made from clay and terracotta, these included small carts, birds, toy monkeys & more.

The Dancing Girl from MohenjoDaro is possibly the first bronze statue. It could have been a creation of a single person or a dedicated team, but results today claim that creativity did boom in that era.

- **Drainage System & Public Litter Bins:** The Indus Valley Civilisation also had advanced sewerage and drainage systems. Several containers strategically located along the street junctions are evident.

Creativity Leads To Transformative Outcomes!

Various inventions, new products, services, spectacular works of art, and novel concepts - all ultimately lead to civilisations growing and evolving. Creativity is thus a necessary step for progress and has had a long history.

Did you know that it is creativity that helped Apple top the Boston Consulting Group's list of "The Most Innovative Companies" for 11 years in a row?

The reason why creativity plays such a role in business is that it's a differentiator. Tucker Marion, an associate professor at Northeastern University's D'Amorc-McKim School of Business, himself said so.

Today, creativity can help find inventive solutions to old problems. You can use it at your workplace for your benefit and that of your business.

Be it language, art, science, technology, education, or environment, creativity helps everyone!

However, we can get stuck with the context of "creativity" and blind spots on how, where and when.

There are times when we struggle for ideas, but nothing appears. And there are times we keep living in our heads, cherishing our alternative creative world, ignoring reality. If you have been in one of these similar situations, it is okay! You are not an exception! We come across many such incidents and experts.

How Many Times Have You Been Lost In Your Creative Spark?

Do you know what powers a creative mind? Imagination! It helps our creative thinking always be on the go. From planning dinner to envisioning an upcoming vacation, we routinely rely on our imaginations to picture what the future might look like. Humans are such alluring creatures — we can even envision experiences that haven't yet occurred.

How often do you have to be creative in your personal and professional life?

Think about it.

A marketing person uses creativity to sell the latest model of car.

A parent uses creativity to help the child finish his new science project.

A makeup artist uses creativity to help the bride look like her swoon-worthy self.

A mechanical engineer uses creativity to design a new technology for his machine.

An author uses creativity to write a new book.

Ultimately, everyone is expressing their creativity and imagination through some activity or the other.

When we hear the word 'creativity' as a noun, we instantly relate it to artistic work, painting, theatre, movies, craftsmanship, music, or sports.

But, as Twyla Tharp puts it,

"Creativity is not just for artists. It's for business people looking for a new way to close a sale. It's for engineers trying to solve a problem. It's for parents who want their children to see the world in more than one way."

Business? Are we sure?

Think about it - every business wants to grow and expand while surpassing the competition, yet only a few can. Why? Because we need to bring something new to the market to grow. And you can't build something new using the same archaic methods.

An organisation has to be fast, flexible and adaptable to change. It needs to bring something different and help customers achieve desired goals.

Can all this happen without creativity and imagination? No!

Using Creativity In Business

One often debated topic is the competence of creativity. Is it by birth, i.e., not everyone can have it? Or is it a virtue that you can develop and nurture further, one that is present deep within everyone? Whatever your belief, your business will need the support of creative souls who understand how it works.

Let's understand that with an example of typical forms of art - music and paintings.

You might know that an orderly, appreciative painting or a musical enthrallment comes out of chaos. That's a non-linear process through thinking and applying thoughts of imagination. This leads to the curious question, do we live in an orderly, predictable environment of business or entrepreneurship?

As per Teresa Amabile, a professor at Harvard Business School,

"Creativity doesn't have any algorithm or framework of rules to arrive at an expected outcome, but just deeper imagination."

Similarly, a business environment doesn't have any algorithm to address volatility or dynamics to live and thrive. If any business problem or situation can get programmed or set up algorithmically, it gets purely mechanical with its rules.

Google recently completed an eye-opening analysis of innovations done there. Its founders tracked the progress of ideas that they had backed versus ideas that got executed in the ranks without support from above. Eventually, they discovered a higher success rate in the latter category.

Similarly, it was noted that Philip Rosedale, the founder and chairman of Linden Lab, the fast-growing company that manages Second Life, gives most workers enormous autonomy. They believe that the greatest successes come from the worker's own initiatives.

3 Ways You Can Develop & Nurture Creativity-

1. **Be Curious:** Psychologists have compiled a large body of research on the many benefits of curiosity. It increases perseverance and grit while boosting mental and physical energy by 20% in addition to happiness.

    The combination of these things with the knowledge received as a result of being curious helps the brain connect a variety of dots. Thus, making way for creativity and innovation.

2. **Aim for Continuous Improvement:** Revolutionary creative ideas won't always just come to you. You can make that easy by allocating time for thinking. But do not stop there. Repeating, rehearsing and creating discipline will surely improve creativity skills.

3. **Count on Your Gut:** Consider your gut to be "the teacher inside." Get acquainted with your inner self, even if you get vague answers. Register them in your conscious mind or document them in a notepad.

Remember, each person's abilities are unique. Some may be in tune with their Gut Voice, while others may not. The idea is to slowly build awareness and find creative answers from within.

Finally, creativity is an interplay of "Will, Strength and Joy."

3C➔C Model of Creativity

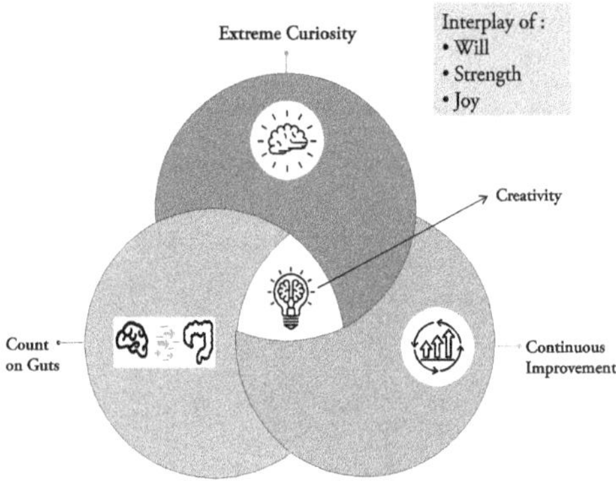

Can We Make Creativity Easy And Contagious For Organisations?

There are various definitions of creativity.

The simplest being-

Something that is created out of applied imagination. Something useful and valuable for the task or situation on hand, where the task is heuristic in nature.

Here, Heuristic means an incomplete guideline or rule of thumb, and it offers no clear path.

While creativity is an applied imagination, it can be useful for INVENTION and INNOVATION too. It can help solve some of the intriguing challenges every business faces and enhance user experiences. Look at successful products and services such as Amazon and Uber. Their story shows how we can turn a new concept into commercial success for widespread use.

Even Indian companies like Shaadi.com are fantastic examples. The world's largest matrimonial service has been recognised as the 'Most Innovative Company in India, 2011' by Fast Company, USA.

Now don't go searching for a sensational or life-changing idea!

Remember what the co-founder of Airbnb says.

"Had we tried to think of a good idea, we **wouldn't** *have been able to think of a* **good idea.** *You just have to* **find the solution** *for a problem in your own life."*

~Brian Chesky, Co-Founder of Airbnb

Just focus on the key elements of growth — creativity, invention, and innovation. They are all interrelated and necessary. Also, they are not just about getting the business started but also sustaining the companies after they have reached a certain recognizable or global scale.

It's time you use these tips and create a profound impact on your business with creativity. Let's not get overwhelmed by terminologies like "Creativity", "invention", and "Innovation" anymore!

With the above approach, you can see that creativity is an integral part of the business. And that at varied functions such as product, processes, organization structure, sales, and go-to-market approach.

Knowingly or unknowingly, Creativity gets developed and deployed at multiple levels in organizations. It won't be wrong to say that **Creativity can be the currency of the 21st century.**

The prosperity of any country depends on its ability to create new ideas, processes, and solutions, more so in the healthcare sector.

Let's look at a recent example of emerging creativity.

A number of hospitals, such as the Boston Children's Hospital, use 3D operating models that allow surgeons to practice complex operations before they walk into the operating room.

Another compelling example is the healthcare set-up RDMD which uses AI to analyze data from medical records to find commonalities in rare diseases, further selling this data to pharmaceutical companies, so they create cutting-edge faster treatments.

You see, India has emerged as a most promising and progressive healthcare sector in recent times. The healthcare crisis post-COVID-19 led to many people fostering new ideas and forcing radical change.

Such a change happened in the field of telemedicine, as 100 healthcare specialists came together to launch a nationwide platform called 'Swasth'. It was focused on COVID care with an aim to remotely connect patients to healthcare providers.

Creativity thrives at all levels when the organizational environment and policies attract and nurture talents actively. Having said that, organizational policies should not be a hindrance to individual creativity to spring up.

Creativity is driven by the need to survive and sustain.

New creative ideas contribute not just to individuals but society as a whole. For instance, the eLocust3 smartphone app was created to address the issue of desert locust outbreaks in Asia and Africa. The app monitors and quickly detects one of the most dangerous migratory beast species in the world. It combines the latest developments in information communication and satellite technologies for early warning systems.

The development of a new normal product, in this case, a solution for famers, was made possible through creativity.

Inner Sources of Creativity

What do you think is our source of creativity?

Our most reliable inner sources of creativity are-

1. **Intuition**, or gut feeling, which comes out as the first response without any conscious reasoning or series of over-analyses in the game.

   Intuitive responses have been leveraged in many important business decisions to help get positive business results. (For instance, many business houses started exploring huge investments for Carbon Neutrality targets during 2019-21).

   As they say, when it comes to innovation, trust your intuition.

   Cognitive science tells us that discoveries and decisions are made largely unconsciously. First comes emotion, not thought. Emotions come before and influence

rational understanding. Neuroscientist Antonio Damasio explained this peculiarity through a revolutionary experiment known as Iowa Gambling Task, designed to improve innovation and real-life decisions in business.

2. The quality of **Will** to take responsibility to fulfil the imagined future or big picture through creative actions.

This *'will'* bring a compelling vision for the future. Visionary leaders, world-class athletes, Nobel laureates, and eminent business personalities have started their journeys, overcome obstacles, and handled disappointments by virtue of their will.

Eventually, they **tasted success.**

You might have heard of the Marshmallow experiment.

Any explanation of "Will" is incomplete without mentioning the famous Marshmallow experiment.

The experiment was a series of studies on delayed gratification in the late 1960s and early 70s, led by Stanford University professor Walter Mischel. In these studies, a child was offered a choice between one small reward provided immediately and two small rewards if the child waited for a short period (approximately 15 minutes), during which the tester left the room and returned. The reward was a Marshmallow.

As this was a longitudinal study, the researchers did several follow-ups over a period of time and found that children who waited longer for the marshmallow

tended to have better life outcomes, as measured by their SAT scores or financial strength as well as better health, measured by standard medical tests.

While we need to possess many attributes to attain success in business, Will is the power that allows us to imagine and achieve set goals.

3. The *Joy* of creativity through iterative difficulties brings a sense of fulfilment.

People experience joy upon realizing their creative potential and applying their minds towards a purpose in solving a challenge or fixing it. Let me share an interesting example here.

Do you have an account on Instagram?

How much do you access it?

We all know that the Instagram app was started as a site for sharing images with followers on the web.

One of the founders, Kevin Systrom, narrated his experience. Initially, when he thought of setting up a site for photos in Silicon Valley, people thought he was crazy. They had a weird look and asked; you left your job at Google to do what? Why are you working on photos? Photos have already been covered by Flickr and Facebook.

Despite the cold feedback, he decided to set up the project. He said that he had already left his job and wanted to create something of his own. The joy of creating something different helped him achieve

success. Today, Instagram has 1.38 billion users across the world.

4. **Strength** is the fourth element of creativity.

To withstand hurdles and setbacks and handle them as common encounters amidst the critic in you and outside, it is necessary to harness the strength within. This is necessary to overcome fears of failures piling up and masking the thought process.

Business people leverage strengths to be *new* and *different.* And that works right for them, as they are willing to take risks and overcome fears.

5. **Compassion** to bring out creativity within the self and from others around.

This comes from recognizing one's own ability and appreciating and motivating others within the team. If there is a bottleneck in organizational creativity, it might be at the top of the bottle.

When business leaders behave creatively and compassionately, they promote creative thinking in employees. A creative person takes novel approaches to interactions, showing personal connections and similar feelings which surprise clients and co-workers, further enhancing the business.

Getting creativity into a Business environment means you have the perfect lever to sustain and thrive.

Let's understand some of the valued insights from different sections.

Famous Personalities Speak On Creativity

"Creativity is seeing the same thing but thinking differently."

~Dr. Abdul Kalam (Famous Scientist from India)

Thomas Alva Edison; Inventor of the Incandescent filament bulb.

Once, an assistant of Thomas Alva Edison in the laboratory asked him why he was so persistent even after efforts on the light bulb (filament) failed thousands of times.

His response to the question was, "I didn't understand the question". *"I have not failed; I've just found 10000 ways that won't work".* This means in his mind, he hadn't failed even once!

Edison always believed in having more creative ideas than just one because the first idea may not be the best idea. He would always encourage more quantities and have a weekly quota for himself and the team too.

Albert Szent; Discoverer of Vitamin-C

"Creativity consists of looking at the same thing as everyone else and thinking something different."

Steve Jobs; Famous inventor with great ideas in the field of computers and smart mobile phones.

"Creativity is just having enough dots to connect, to connect experiences and to synthesize new things."

Creativity is just connecting things. When you ask creative people how they did something, they feel a little guilty because they didn't really do it, they just saw something. It seemed obvious to them after a while. That's because they were able to connect experiences they've had and synthesize new things.

Peter Drucker (Management consultant, educator, author)

"I always stress to my clients that they have to be ready to change. You have to be prepared to make your innovation obsolete. But many companies aren't prepared to do that."

Does this perhaps indicate that man has a spirit of creation?

The honest answer is a *high level of creativity stimulates the economy and promotes growth and welfare.*

Fresh perspectives/Thoughts To Ponder On

Delivering affordable and quality services to India's billion-plus population presents enormous challenges. Could creativity be a way out for a nation like this?

Can creativity be a possible solution to ensure quick, more efficient, and sustainable methods to address India's widespread needs?

<table>
<tr><td colspan="1" align="center">Action Plan for the Week</td></tr>
<tr><td>Think about one amateur creative idea that you want to execute today.</td></tr>
<tr><td>There is a situation at work. You have been stuck in that situation. Now, instead of complaining or getting irritated, put compassion into the problem. Feel positive for all the people involved there. Ponder over the feelings for 5 minutes in silence. Your subconscious mind will bring the 'aha' solution today.</td></tr>
<tr><td>Whether you are a leader (at work or home), take the first step of fostering creativity in your meeting room or drawing room.</td></tr>
<tr><td>Remember, intrinsic motivation or willpower is important to promote creativity, as motives are essential in real-world settings.</td></tr>
<tr><td>Just for today, announce a reward for all those who will wear the thinking hat. While you acknowledge the strength of creative people, it will be equally reinforced in you.</td></tr>
<tr><td>Lastly, make a list of characteristics that will support creativity and propose new ideas at the workplace.</td></tr>
</table>

Summary

Demystifying the concept of creativity – from its origin, definition, and usefulness to its role in business successes today is the essence of this chapter.

Interestingly, history traces creativity to the times of the Indus Valley civilization, where a plethora of inventions (for the benefit of society) elucidated people's creative genius even in those times.

Creativity has a wider connotation than is commonly believed and cannot be merely confined to the arts, painting, music, or sculpturing. And, definitely, it is innovation that has illuminated the paths of countless organizations, helping them optimize profitability to reach the top!

Now the question is, is creativity inherited, or can it be learned?

Nature versus nurture! Creativity is a dizzying mix of genes and the environment; fortunately, a trait that can be acquired/developed. A better explanation of this can be garnered by the 3C model, which attributes creativity to 3 essential factors - extreme curiosity, continuous improvement, and count on guts.

Undoubtedly, there is an inner source of creativity in each of us. We just need to hone these inherent traits to witness astounding results. Intuition, will, joy, strength, and compassion are some of those inner sources.

By far, in the business scenario, too, innovative ideas happen as a result of a new combination of old elements! Transformation or a positive change is the key element here, noticeable in the world of business today. All that, combined with agility, flexibility, and imagination, certainly ensures victory!

Chapter II

Sowing the Seeds of Creativity

In the previous chapter, we talked about several surprising elements of creativity, specifically relating to business. **We understand creativity is not just in art, music, painting, and sculptures but in the business environment too.** The business segment is also an adobe for fostering creativity to enhance user experience and solve many of the problems around. A carpenter, plumber, engineer, programmer, and even a medicine practitioner embraces creativity in delivering the best experiences.

> *"All things are created twice, first mentally; then physically.*
> *The key to creativity is to begin with the end in mind,*
> *with a vision and a blueprint of the desired result."*
>
> **~Stephen R. Covey**

In this chapter, we shall understand the various methods to foster creativity in organizations and at individual levels. But before we discover these methods, let's find out what led to creativity's rise in organizations; how it became the game-changer it is today.

⚱

Nike's efforts made 48% of players use its shoes.

Nike, a world-famous brand for sneakers and active wear - when launching their Epic React shoes in 2018, brought an ultimate immersive experience of an augmented reality based video game where players could try the Epic React on for size. It resulted in 48% of the players purchasing the shoes. You see, a creative step in marketing helped boost the sales of a new product in just a few months.

Amazon tripled its revenues since 2002 to $13 billion with such creativity.

The key was, giving customers choices, not just from products, but also between buying from Amazon directly or from outside vendors on the site. Amazon's new digital offerings, such as e-books, videos, and music, presented a fresh menu of options. Because of its commitment to world-class customer service, Amazon developed a range of innovative tools to help users track packages and quickly return or exchange ordered items, bringing simplicity and convenience to their online shopping experience.

Samsung brought the first foldable OLED screen.

In collaboration with a game company called Reactrix, Samsung creatively designed a TV that lets viewers move what's on the screen with the wave of a hand. Originality and Innovation thus became game changers for Samsung.

Another market leader in terms of Creativity and Innovation is Apple.

The company's main purpose is to create products that enrich people's daily lives. It doesn't develop just product categories but continually innovates within them. When the iPhone was introduced in 2007, Steve Jobs devoted only six seconds to its camera. Since then, the iPhone camera technology has contributed to the photography industry with High dynamic range imaging (2010), panorama photos (2012), True Tone flash (2013), optical image stabilization (2015), the dual-lens camera (2016), portrait mode (2016), portrait lighting (2017), and night mode (2019).

Reports say that iPhone generated $205.5 Bn in revenue in 2022; meaning iPhone represented approximately 52% of the total revenue of $3934.3 Bn for the year.

"I knew that if I failed, I wouldn't regret that, but I knew the one thing I might regret is not trying."

~Jeff Bezos, founder and CEO of Amazon

Let's recall we started this journey of creativity with un-mechanized but heuristic techniques. Though many approaches are touched upon, it doesn't necessarily mean there's some need to follow them to the point. We are letting multiple degrees of freedom spark creativity engines.

What Curtails Creative Changes From Childhood To Adulthood?

As human beings, we are strong in our connection to the external world with our 5 senses: sight, hearing, smell, taste, and touch.

Our sense of self values, beliefs, memories (positive or negative experiences), and neural programming all act as filters that moderate or manipulate sensory inputs. Then it is our mind that processes these sensory inputs into feelings or perceptions.

In short, it is our thoughts that create realities around us, and so, if we can change our thoughts to new versions, we can create new realities. However, in everyday life, we are too immersed in routines like walking, showering, dressing, cooking, or driving a car, most of which happen unconsciously. These mundane activities take away a lot of our time, due to which several doors of creativity simply close behind us.

In order to generate new creative ideas, we must do the routine chores differently. For example, if you have followed the same route to your office for many years, it is time to find a new route. Change the direction; find a new path so that you create new realities both in your mind and life.

Lack of Awareness and Attentiveness

You would agree that a musician must learn about the notes before tuning a new song. A medical practitioner can invent new ways of treating diseases only when he knows the basics of anatomy. Can we then learn anything without paying attention to the most crucial and core areas that form the basis of that subject? No!

Now we all know that attention is a limited resource.

There is so much distraction in our day-to-day lives. We are continuously struggling to focus in one direction. Paying

attention requires some extra effort these days, simply because our awareness is scattered in all directions. From social media to that colleague who cannot stop gossiping, there are many snatchers of our attention.

However, creativity starts by paying greater attention to things around us or processes around us where we seek some improvements.

Creativity is more likely where the environment is free from rigid cultures and structures. Let's say there are two artists. One tells you an idea for a great painting, but he does not paint it. The other has the same idea and paints it. You could easily say the second man is a great creative artist. But could you say the same thing for the first man? Obviously not. He is merely a talker, not a painter.

This is where we need to break the rigidity or stereotypes in the environment. A great thinker can be only responsible for generating ideas while you hire an executioner separately who makes it happen. We need to introduce a new way of doing things.

Psychology Of The "Creative Type" Some people are extremely creative right from the start. Their Kindergarten teachers will testify. Their naïve curiosity brings questions such as-

- "Why can you see through glass?"
- "Why is there a hole in a doughnut?"
- "Why is the grass green?"

This kind of questioning attitude produces creative freshness in a young mind. As the child grows older, they bring an integrative mechanism of adult creativity to their workplace. In fact, when you are creative, you display an ability to adapt to almost any situation and to make do with whatever is at hand to reach your goals.

Another important factor that can be observed in the creative type is - you can be smart yet naive at the same time.

Creative people combine playfulness and discipline or responsibility and irresponsibility. They alternate between imagination or fantasy and a rooted sense of reality.

Great art and great science involve a leap of imagination into a world that is different from the present. But this "escape" is not into never-never land, in isolation. You could get an idea even in the thick of crowds or sitting on the sidelines and observing the passing show. Once you reach home, you pen it down and execute it.

Simple as that!

Creative Context With Rapid Development

Creativity is an integral part of what makes us human. Even though there is rapid development in the application of computers in the artificial intelligence domain with respect to sophisticated data crunching, we still agree that human creative skills are of the highest levels.

A 2016 World Economic Forum report concluded that creativity would be the third most important skill in the workplace by 2020. We have stepped into 2023, and I am sure you can clearly see the changes at your workplace.

Creativity is the skill of the future. In fact, in the next five years, a typical CV or Resume will look very different. Your experience and competency will be valued more on the basis of thinking, creativity, and problem-solving skills (basically your Creative IQ) rather than computer programming, something that will be done by AI at a fraction of the cost.

When we get engaged in certain creative activities, we wish to deliver the highest performance of our abilities. Creative tasks always help us to offer better insights and enhance the quality of our living. Today, humankind is experiencing challenges like never before - terrorism, pollution, poverty, and lack of food, areas where creativity can help us to be better problem solvers.

*"The way to get started is to quit talking
and begin doing."*

~Walt Disney, founder of Disney

While we agree about creativity being an inherent quality of human beings, the only question that arises is why aren't we consistently creative.

The aptest answer is our creativity has been curtailed by our busy minds, a negative judgment about ourselves and from others, and our fears.

A study published in Psychological Science found that when our mind is too encumbered by mental taxation, and so we are less likely to seek out novelty and creativity. You see, if these elements are curtailing our originality, how can we be more creative when we address these inhibitions?

Thought Patterns That Bring Creativity To The Fore

In the following sections, we cover important topics about creating competency to support creativity. Please remember, *"Creativity cannot be accomplished by brute force. It requires a specific breeding ground"*.

1. Extreme Curiosity

"I have no special talent, I am only passionately curious."

~Albert Einstein

As a child, we have been curious to understand everything around us and learn more about the unknown. However, this curiosity trait diminishes as we grow up due to our social environment, structure, and formal education systems.

Well-understood and managed curiosity propels us to learn more about things, leading to creativity. Together, curiosity

and learning a wide array of multi-faceted topics lead us to develop a better ability to create high-quality solutions and overcome the challenges around us.

- Curiosity helps you become proactive. It helps us see the problems differently and find alternate solutions.

- Being curious allows us to generate many ideas. It makes us recognize patterns and solutions, plus enhances "possibilities", thereby shifting from "limitations".

- Curiosity shifts you to become active, not getting bored, being busy, and having new things to catch up on.

- It boosts our commitment and vigour for tasks on hand, never letting us get bored.

- With creativity comes a deep understanding of how things work and multiple perspectives, which make them more efficient and useful.

- It brings clarity of thoughts with more answers on-hand, stimulating us to achieve goals effectively.

How to Spark Curiosity?

- **Question things:** A curious child keeps questioning for long. This questioning mindset leads to more clarity and solutions for problems around. Their questions may be called dumb, but children continue to ask and get a deeper understanding of issues. Thus, generating more ideas.

Give a child a little block or a feather or pen cap as their toy, and they will surprise you. They won't say that what you gave them isn't a toy. They will twist, rotate, throw, pick it up again, and do every possible thing with this object and entertain themselves. No wonder kids are creative, and their minds are filled up to the brim with ideas all the time. Don't you think sometimes it is essential for us adults to act like a child?

- **Do something different:** Doing the same set of activities monotonously every day limits our ability to generate ideas. Try doing different things like taking the unusual route back home, brushing with the other hand, watching a different web series rather than the one you have watched 10 times, talking to new acquaintances, and getting to know how your colleague spends their days.

- If there is a new health plan coming and you are afraid you won't be able to do it, volunteer, for it anyhow. You will eventually settle into the new feeling and understand that there is nothing to fear.

- **Conquer your fear:** Most people are afraid of trying anything new at their job for various reasons. After all, we are creatures of habit, and change can move us out of our comfort zone. Therefore, we feel content with the existing work rather than trying new strategies that could probably give a boost to our company in the market.

"The oldest and strongest emotion of mankind is fear, and the oldest and strongest kind of fear is the fear of the unknown."

~H.P. Lovecraft

Note that the more curious you are, the less afraid you will be. Focus on the positive outcomes when trying something new. For e.g., if you are trying to sing for the first time - imagine there is a crowd applauding you and giving you a standing ovation on the stage.

- **Move beyond being "bored":** If you are looking at something and feel bored, you are not looking hard enough. Read a magazine that you have never tried, passionately watch some of the people around you, and list some peculiar actions. Phrases like "that's the way it's always done" are dangerous and feed drudgery. If you are thinking this way or hearing your colleagues use such statements, it's a sign that creativity is stifled at your workplace.

2. Deep Attention And Observation

*"If you see in any given situation only what everybody
else can see, you can be so much a representative
of your culture that you are a victim of it."*

~S.I. Harakawa, Semanticist

Deep attention to what we see, hear ("listen" to be precise), feel, taste and smell can offer deeper insights into our surroundings.

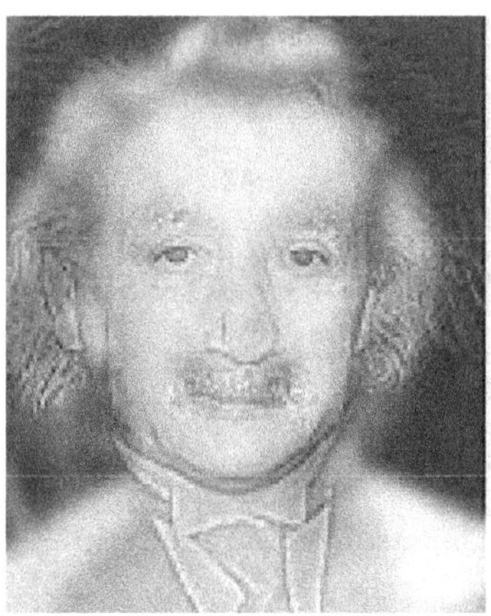

For example, refer to the image above; can you recognize this famous person?

At first glance, most of us see a photograph of Albert Einstein, one of the famous creative geniuses of the time.

Possibly, if you would like to see another famous person, you may need to move a bit away from the image or take off your glasses if you use one. When the image is out of focus, you can see the photograph of the famous Hollywood celebrity Marilyn Monroe. The image is able to offer a different perspective when your focus and attention are changed.

Michael Bilich, General Manager of a famous US leasing firm, puts it this way: *Every single thing you do not only recognizes what you're doing but also the purpose for which you are doing it. And all of a sudden, you will start to see things opening up all over the place.*

As we start paying attention, we get to realize the beauty from within, our own creative resource!

Similarly, sharpening our ears for "Listening" instead of "hearing" is the need. We have a natural tendency to hear conversations, songs, and chirping birds without paying much attention. When we shift this hearing tendency to a listening mode, we understand and appreciate content much deeper.

If you are in a sales job, actively listening to customers for issues, challenges, and tasks on hand, will help you offer a better solution to them and enhance their confidence in your genuineness and emerging solutions.

3. Stop Being Judgemental

As children, we used to carry fewer belief systems and more curiosity and wonder than as adults. Ask your parents and elders, and they'll tell you how you could sometimes be a pain in the neck with your series of questions.

Growing up, we get conditioned, and our inner voice of judgement emerges. Our world becomes full of knowledge, great experiences, bad news, and comparisons, steering us away from stepping into unfamiliar topics and terrains. We start ignoring problems and passively submit to circumstances.

People in general, or even employees, are reluctant to share their ideas because they worry that people will mock and ridicule what they don't understand. They are afraid of the implications of the possible future.

Here's what we need to understand.

Our internal voice of judgment is characterized by a habitual, comfortable, and programmed attitude. These are

thought patterns that block our creative thinking. They make us focus on our weaknesses when we should consider failure and missteps as necessary stepping stones to new approaches, products, and services that help us grow.

Look at the image below. Observe closely.

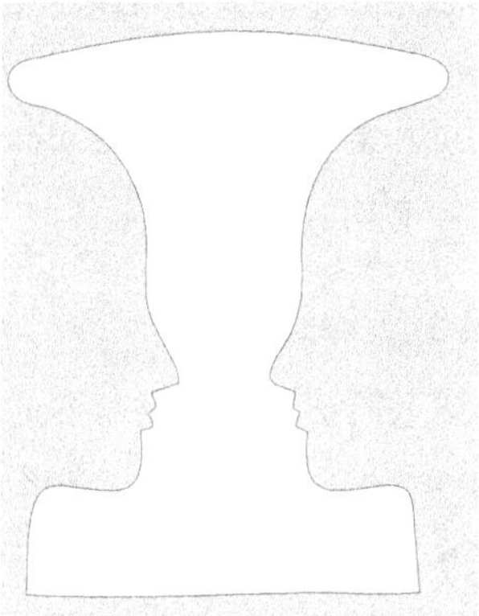

What do you see?

Some of you will see a vase. Some will see two people facing each other (in the image).

As a viewer, we have a mental choice of two interpretations, each of which is valid. Often, we see only one of them and realize the second, valid interpretation after some time or prompting. What we will see first is a result of our inner programming.

Now, when you are actively pursuing your creative skills, it is important to view or interpret all the perspectives that a situation presents. Adapting such a habit will help us overcome situational bias while creating new ways of addressing problems.

4. Redirect Your Creative Thought Process

Does creative thinking happen spontaneously, or can we deliberately direct the process?

Neuroscience says that relaxing the filter in our brains by letting our minds wander—a process governed by the hippocampus and default network—can allow new ideas to float in our minds. But serendipity and spontaneity alone do not guarantee either novelty or usefulness. We often need to redirect our thought processes away from what we already know and think hard about whether our ideas will actually work.

Creative thinking involves the interplay of the brain's default and executive control networks, and these connections allow us to spontaneously generate ideas and critically evaluate them.

So, let's put them into two categories - Creativity By Default & Creativity By Design

Ask yourself, do you purposely sit to generate ideas, or do they appear randomly in your life?

5. The Need For Discipline

The primary element of creativity is the Creative Impulse Itself. And sometimes, it is important to emphasize how creative ideas will fit into the requirements.

First, we start by identifying a dozen new ideas. Then we put together these ideas into practical reality while also overcoming challenges.

The second step needs to happen without procrastination. Acting on small, simple steps every day can lead to big achievements.

You may have observed at your workplace that many times a brainstorming meeting ends with many ideas and no conclusive thoughts. Delaying tactics, stalling ideas, and temporizing the process can all lead to creative dissatisfaction in the future. So 'Discipline' becomes a mandatory part of the creative process.

Some Quotes From Famous Personalities

The principal goal of education in schools should be creating men and women who are capable of doing new things, not simply repeating what other generations have done; men and women who are creative, inventive, and discoverers, who can be critical and verify, and not accept, everything they are offered.

~Jean Piaget

Freethinkers are those who are willing to use their minds without prejudice and without fearing to understand things that clash with their own customs, privileges, or beliefs. This state of mind is not common, but it is essential for critical thinking.

~Leo Tolstoy

You have a brain and mind of your own.
Use it, and reach your own decisions.

~Napoleon Hill

Follow the path of the unsafe, independent thinker. Expose your ideas to the danger of controversy. Speak your mind and fear less the label of a crackpot than the stigma of conformity.

~Thomas J. Watson, Sr.

The important thing in science is not so much to obtain new facts as to discover new ways of thinking about them.

~Sir William Bragg

Fresh perspectives/Thoughts To Ponder On

How can you unleash creativity in spite of restrictions?

Is creativity harder than everyday chores?

Action Plan for the Week
Sometimes it is necessary to act like a child. Kids are creative, and their minds are full of ideas all the time.
For one day, become 'proactive', see the problems differently and find alternate solutions.
Pick up one household chore that you will do consistently and be creative each time. For example, cooking or dusting at home.
For this week, focus on "Listening" rather than "Hearing". Listen to other people. Evaluate and respond patiently instead of reacting.
Stop focusing on your weaknesses. Consider failure and missteps as a necessary stepping stone to new approaches in creativity. Make a list of failures and work towards it one at a time.

Summary

Delving further into the realms of creativity, this chapter provides a deeper understanding by providing the best ways

to uncover our creative genius. Innumerable business houses touching the pinnacles of success, medical breakthroughs, and instances from our everyday lives is proof enough that treading the path of creativity guarantees triumph in any field.

On the basis of studies conducted on innovation, vital factors augmenting creativity are:

a. Doing routine activities differently, avoiding repetition; embracing change

b. Awareness and the power of observation

c. Attention to detail; Concentration

d. Flexibility, openness to different experiences

Finally, it is a universal principle that nothing can be achieved without discipline, originality, and passion. Hence, paying heed to all of these points will help lead to a win-win situation.

As in other life events, our thinking patterns play a significant role in generating innovative ideas. An important component of thought is `curiosity' or the eagerness to know. Humans are gifted with this virtue, an ideal characteristic for problem-solving.

So whenever you are wrestling with an idea, donning your creativity hat is the sure-shot solution for the minutest of problems to major ones.

Also highlighted here are reasons that mar creativity - negative opinions about ourselves and others, being judgemental, fear, and preoccupations of the mind.

Chapter III

Tools to Unleash Creativity – CLAD Model to get Smarter

Just take a minute for yourself, close your eyes, and observe your thoughts.

What did you discover?

We "do" things in life so much that we forget to take time to think creatively. On the surface level, we are constantly engaging, travelling, interpreting, communicating, and running. There are a gazillion things flashing across your mind at the speed of light, like multitasking, sending emails while eating, doing meetings while travelling, and checking social media while cleaning. Reading, thinking, walking, brainstorming - everything's happening at the same time.

Now, multitasking might make you feel like - "Oh, I'm so productive and powerful."

However, research conducted at Stanford University says that multitasking or mental juggling is problematic as it kills your performance and may even damage your brain.

What about your creativity?

Amidst all this work, when are you giving your mind time to relax and ignite the creative part of your brain?

Creative thinking doesn't just happen. It's something we need to work on. When we start investing our time and energy into it, creative ideas spring out of core depths.

"I never took a day off in my twenties. Not one."

~Bill Gates, co-founder of Microsoft

As currently, there are many tools available to help people unleash their creativity and develop their inner talents. The following tools can help individuals and organizations bring new opportunities into the business world.

CLAD Model

One of the core abilities of the human mind is the power to think critically yet with imagination and creativity.

CLAD Model stands for *Convergent, Lateral, Aesthetic, and Divergent* thinking process.

Let's explore each one separately.

Divergent and Convergent thinking are two complementary methods to nurture creativity, explore ideas, and work towards goals. Both approaches are necessary and lead to unique solutions.

1. Divergence tools, focused on the generation of as many ideas as possible.

2. Convergence tools strive to analyze, filter and merge ideas in order to select the best ones.

Divergence Tools

Let's say an entire team is sitting in a conference room. And you, as a leader, decide to give an ideation time (a couple of minutes) to everyone. Now, people will try to generate as many ideas as possible during this short time span. So 10 employees and 10 Brains run free and generate as many creative ideas as possible.

Divergent thinking means you are simply using your imagination and generating creative ideas by exploring several possible solutions. This is also known as Creative Thinking or Horizontal Thinking. This type of process occurs in a spontaneous, free-flowing, non-linear environment.

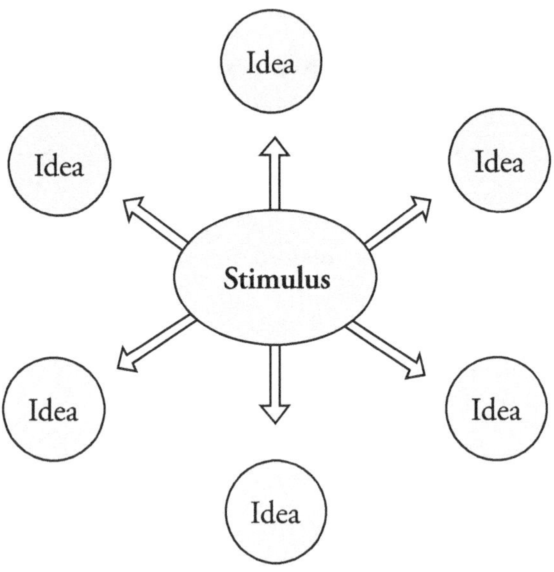

Here are some of the things that happen in divergent thinking -

- We expand the scope of knowledge.

- We generate ideas.

- We engage in possibilities.

- We seek out the unusual.

- We try and combine previously stored information.

- We visualize, imagine, and do free-wheeling with ideas.

A basic rule here is not to criticize or judge new ideas as they come, as negativity is probably the best way to kill creativity. Instead, we figure out new procedures to solve a problem despite existing solutions.

'Diverge', as the name suggests, refers to generating a limitless number of solutions for any given problem, no matter how unrelated they might be, which are then spread on the table to pick out the best one.

One great example of divergent thinking in action is in the early days of Twitter. Twitter took a Minimum Viable Product (MVP) approach to their application. They created an online service without a clear, practical application or market, launched it to see how people would use it, and then refined it. This doesn't mean that it is a bulletproof strategy. In Twitter's case, this worked. In many cases, it might not work. Similarly, many software engineers may use the same techniques to tackle technology challenges with designers.

Convergence Tools

Stepping into this role requires a completely different mindset. A convergent approach involves putting a few ideas together to determine how they are related. To come up with a solution, you must first analyze the situation in depth, organize your ideas, and then come up with a solution.

Convergent thinking is a term coined by Joy Paul Guilford. It is the type of thinking that focuses on coming up with a single, well-established answer to a problem. So you might recognize previously tried-out techniques and reapply them along with the readily stored information.

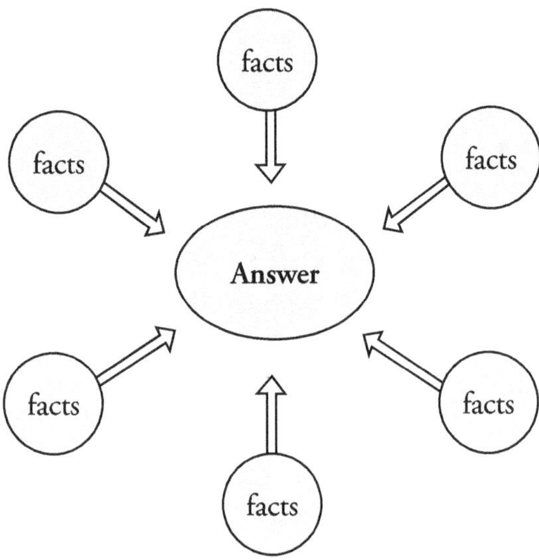

Here are some of the things that happen in convergent thinking -

- We narrow down the topic.

- We rate by criteria.

- We categorize, refine and select.

- We focus on the existing knowledge base instead of finding new ones.

- We use a structural approach.

- We connect all the existing facts to arrive at a decision.

One of the key characteristics of convergent thinking is it helps to find out the best possible answer to any problem, which is accurate most of the time, and no room for ambiguity is left.

The answer is either 100% right or 100% wrong. Essentially, convergent thinking considers the world as Black and/or White, with no other possibilities. For example, according to a convergent thinker, a person can be either sick or healthy. But a divergent thinker would regard a person to be both sick and healthy. The person can be under great stress mentally but perfectly fit physically.

Let me share convergent thinking through a big historical example.

On October 14th, 1957, Russians launched Sputnik into space, thereby initiating the space race. The success of the Russians in technology came as a bolt to the United States. In response, the country set up the National Aeronautics and Space Administration a year later.

In the first half of the 1960s, then President John F. Kennedy sent letters to Wernher von Braun and other key persons in the aerospace industry. He wanted to know how the U.S. could defeat Russia in the space race. After his famous speech where he promised to get a man transported to the moon and also ensure his safe return, nearly 400,000 NASA staff and contractors came in to join hands as a cohesive team and achieve one of the best events of history in under a decade.

Kennedy utilized data and facts to find out how the U.S. could defeat the Russians in the space conquest. That was an example of chiefly convergent thinking. This remarkable feat called for the making of many new technologies to design and manufacture rockets, lunar modules, spacesuits, and other necessary equipment requiring a considerable amount of divergent thinking.

Now, you might think that divergent thinking is more closely related to creativity. However, both processes are required to harness this skill. These two complement each other. Consider them to be like two sides of a coin. They are completely in contrast with each other yet extremely important in our daily lives. Divergent thinking helps you generate novel ideas, whereas convergent thinking will help you evaluate these ideas and finally select one.

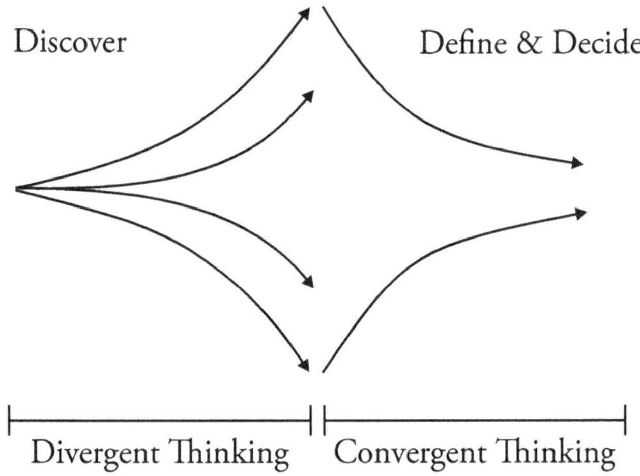

Now, in the CLAD Model, L stands for Lateral Thinking.

In the face of fast-changing trends and fierce competition, there comes a time when you have to adopt both Convergent and Divergent Thinking processes, and eureka lateral thinking is born!

It is a deliberate, systematic process of using your ability to think in a different way.

1. Shattering the myths around creative thinking.

2. Shifting from the single focus on problems.

3. Develop your own creative task list.

4. Learning 'how to use concepts for breeding new ideas.

5. Using random inputs to create new connections.

6. Turning provocative ideas into practical solutions.

7. Transforming starter ideas into workable ideas.

Next time you want to create a fast, effective tool to help yourself or your team, switch to Lateral Thinking.

Last but not least, A stands for Aesthetics.

The ability to appreciate and respond to beauty is referred to as 'Aesthetic Sense'. Although beauty can be subjective, there are certain things, such as harmony, excellence, and intelligence, that are considered beautiful by everyone.

When we create a product or service, we appreciate and analyze it as a work of art. When we start paying attention to aesthetics, we develop into mature and creative adults capable of bringing change and innovation to transform the future.

Today, companies like Apple often use aesthetics or salient visual attributes to differentiate their products from those of their competitors and also to appeal to customers.

The power of aesthetics is truly amazing. For example, Starbucks has an appealing image that follows them, such as cosy cafes, tasty coffee, and comfortable workspaces, and even the logo is considered aesthetically pleasing. Millions of people purchase Starbucks-based merchandise.

Attractiveness is something that takes a lot of time and skill; it's also something that many people pay attention to, consciously or unconsciously. People get biased when it comes to the visuals they see. So next time you create a new product, pay attention to aesthetics to know its true power.

After the CLAD Model, we will pay attention to more interesting tools that help in amplifying creativity.

Psychological Tools

A study in 2014 found that people tend to be more creative when they are walking rather than when they are sitting down. Some research also showed that regular physical activity could play an important role in boosting and protecting cognitive abilities. Either way, we can say that creativity is not a passive process. Instead, we can keep looking for ways to boost our own creativity. Seek out the things that inspire us to generate new ideas.

Let us discover some psychological tools that spark a creative output in us.

Rewards and Reinforcements

Reinforcers such as salary hikes, bonuses, promotions, variable incomes, flexible work hours, and paid sabbaticals have always

been used as common positive-reinforcement techniques to increase the efficiency of employees. Managers recognize what behaviours should be promoted and carefully design organizational objectives accordingly. Now, how about using the same technique on yourself?

Promise yourself some type of desirable treat as a reward for coming up with a creative solution.

Reward yourself when you are curious about something.

Pamper your mind and body with a Spa or a new dress when you come up with a solution.

It is also important to develop intrinsic <u>motivation that keeps fuelling the creative juices.</u>

Emotional Boundaries

We are all aware that positive emotions are strongly linked to creativity, but research has also found that negative emotional states are also linked to creative thinking. This doesn't mean you should rush out and put yourself in a bad mood just to gain some inspiration. But the next time we experience a negative emotional state, we can dissipate this energy towards solving a problem or accomplishing a task rather than just sitting around with anger.

Meditation

There has been enough research to prove that Meditation is a great relaxation technique. But its benefits extend beyond relaxation.

"A Highly Connected Brain Is A Highly Creative Brain".

~Dr. Roger Sperry, Nobel Prize Winner in 1981

He suggested that creativity is actually a 'whole brain' function. There is a bundle of 200 million nerve fibres connecting the left and right brain hemispheres, upgrading our "corpus callosum" (CC), leading the "whole brain communication". Later a study by the UCLA School of Medicine showed that meditation cranks up the corpus callosum, making it bigger, stronger, thicker, and well-connected. A meditation-supercharged corpus callosum opens the door to what's called the creative 'brain dance'. Thus, by bringing in meditation, you step into 'out of cubicle thinking'.

How Meditation Changed Hollywood's Creativity?

In the early 1980s, Walt Disney was at a creative crossroads. In the hopes of "accessing new creative directions," executives called a high-profile psychotherapist and meditation teacher Dr. Ron Alexander. After seeing the massive creative leaps by those who finished his mindfulness course, the Walt Disney Company adopted mindfulness on a broad scale. In 2007, Google brought a mindfulness course named "Search Inside Yourself. Later, companies like Apple and Nike also followed in their footsteps.

Mind Maps

"Mind maps" is a visual thinking tool. It is one of the great ways to organize thoughts and ideas organically. Let's say you start by picking up a central idea or topic. Now, start writing all the things that embody this central topic. Outline concepts

that are related to this main theme. You can brainstorm to find associations, keywords, images, sub-topics, and basically all the things that are closely related to the topic. Mind maps allow you to take various interconnected trains of thought and put them in one place. In the process, you learn new concepts, boost creativity and improve productivity.

Today, many businesses are using apps such as "Mind Meister", "Mind Genius", "And Mind Manager", which allow them to use diagram templates or create visual cues. Primarily, you are plotting ideas into diagrams, therefore turning complex information into more comprehendible, organized, memorable representations.

But how will you nurture creativity?

Fundamentally our brain processes visual information 60,000 times faster than text. So while creating mind maps, you are sowing the seeds for a creative idea underneath the surface of your brain. Once your mind starts to think, you start capturing information, and your imagination stretches far and wide. Once your imagination is on a roll, ideas start flooding in from all directions. Since all these ideas are represented visually, your brain is able to form more creative associations between them.

Close your eyes and imagine an apple.

What do you see?

Some of you may visualize a round shape, red-coloured, smooth, shiny apple. You may even see a knife or a plate along with it. But it doesn't end there. The train of thought will now take you to a memory where you see yourself or a loved one eating an apple. You may even see the apple vendor or a commercial of apple juice or any memory (in your mind) that has been associated with an apple.

Did you realize how quickly the mind creates an association when it is presented with the smallest visual cue?

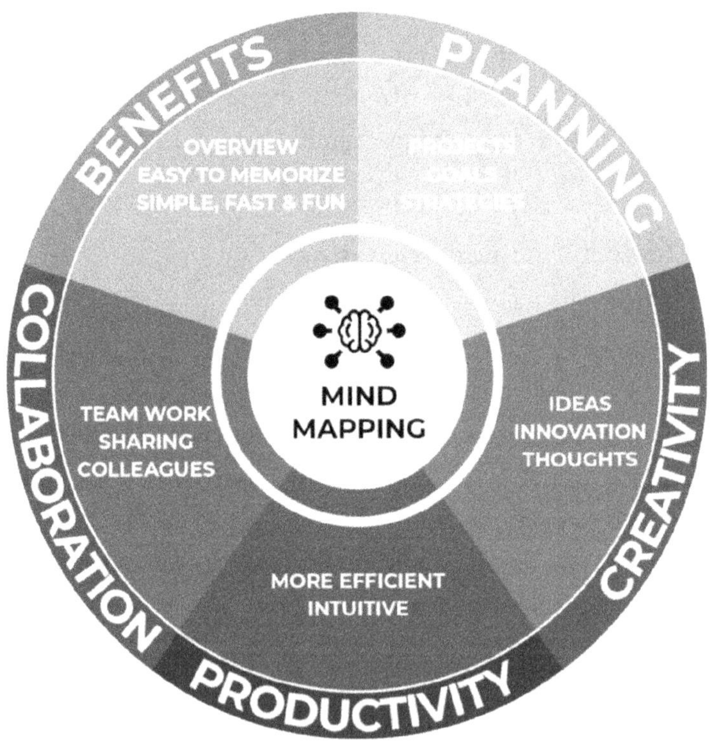

Mind Maps help you expand your creative ideas and turn them into something tangible.

Thinking hat

This is a popular technique used to explore the upsides and downsides of every idea. Created by Edward de Bono, a Maltese physician, psychologist, and philosopher, this approach helps you use the instinctive approach as opposed to habitual ways of thinking. For example, your department conducts an experiment called the Thousand Rupees Test.

Rs. 1000 is freely allocated to the entire team. Next, people are asked to buy a particular idea, whatever they think is worth paying for. After the funds are distributed, the most popular ideas can be easily identified, as those participants will receive most of the money. Since we are rating the ideas, the experiment can also be called idea shopping. Now, some people will buy an idea based on curiosity, while others buy the idea after considering every angle; few people will purchase unique thoughts. A small percentage of people will be buying an idea that others buy in order to be part of a shared understanding.

The question is - Are we able to train our minds to think creatively and communicate in fresh ways?

A group of CEOs was asked, "What is the skill you most value in your people?" (as part of a survey).

They said 'creativity' is the ability to solve problems, come up with new solutions, and use brainpower to figure things out.

Thinking Hat is a system designed to promote creative thinking. It is a tool used to enhance real thinking to make the process more productive and focused. The '6 Thinking

Hats' separates thinking into 6 different roles, each role identified with a coloured symbolic thinking hat. This approach helps to redirect thoughts by mentally switching from one hat to the other.

Let's look at these 6 thinking hats.

1. **White Hat**–stating facts and information, things you already know.

2. **Yellow Hat**–looking at the bright side, being optimistic and positive, adding value and benefits.

3. **Red Hat**–expressing feelings and emotions, reactions, and opinions.

4. **Blue Hat**–managing and controlling, looking at the bigger picture.

5. **Green Hat**– exploring other alternatives and generating new ideas and solutions.

6. **Black Hat**– being realistic and practical, being cautious, finding where things might go wrong, discovering dangers and difficulties.

For example, you can start by grabbing the "Blue Hat" and asking yourself questions such as.

What is our goal?

What is the subject addressed?

Next, you can grab the "Red Hat", express your feelings towards the problem and ask yourself who might be affected by this problem.

Then, you can grab "Yellow" and later "Green Hat" to invent new concepts and solutions.

When we start training our minds to switch from one perspective to another, we generate a new string of ideas (by just switching the caps).

Doodling

Some of history's greatest thinkers of the century, like Steve Jobs, John F. Kennedy, and Henry Ford, have engaged in 'doodling' as a pathway for unlocking creativity. To doodle means to "scribble absentmindedly". So doodling is very different from creating Mind Maps. Here you are liberating your mind from traditional, linear, and linguistic thinking and moving into a more organic thinking space.

For example, a 2009 study from the University of Plymouth found those who doodled during a recorded phone call recalled 29 per cent more information than those who didn't doodle. It helps you to focus and find new solutions. Suppose you are stuck on a project, confused by a problem, or experiencing creative blocks. Just sit down with a pen and paper and start drawing random circles, shapes, and lines while thinking about that specific topic. At this time, this random doodling is stirring neurological pathways of the mind, allowing you to look at information from new angles. The process is visual, written, kinaesthetic, and emotional. Therefore, it enhances recalling and lightens up neural networks that create cognitive breakthroughs.

Digital Tools

Traditional techniques of stimulating creativity have been replaced and enhanced by technology-driven tools, such as virtual rooms, decision cockpits, various communication tools, and interactive dashboards. In particular, the Internet of things (IoT), artificial intelligence (AI), and virtual reality (VR) have an impact on the creativity of entrepreneurs and their teams. For example, the use of the internet has now made it possible for ideas to be sourced from virtually anywhere, going beyond the capabilities of manpower.

Today, AI is used to uncover certain statistics and help determine your interest areas and marketing opportunities far more effectively than compared with traditional practices.

Platforms such as Adobe, Instagram, and YouTube allow future professionals, artists, and amateurs to post content on these platforms and test the market for future business endeavours. That means we can express ourselves and showcase talent without bounds and even connect with audiences that have similar interests.

Instagram, one of the most popular social media platforms, works on the S-O-R framework. 'S' stands for stimulus, which means you are generating perceptions of creativity. 'O' stands for organisms, which means a positive response by your followers. 'R' stands for a response, which means gaining their commitment and interactions.

Now, can you say affirmatively that technology is boosting your creativity?

We are all capable of being creative, though, with the application of the correct tools, our innate skills can be enhanced and harnessed. Let me explain this with an example below.

Digital tools have helped people to 'speak' simultaneously. Imagine you're in a meeting with 10 individuals, discussing the strategy for a big project. During a face-to-face interaction, each person will have limited time to share their ideas. Only one person can speak at a time for an order to be maintained, which means each person would be allocated only six minutes at the most to share their thoughts within one hour. A cap is placed on the number of ideas that can be generated.

Now, take that meeting to an electronic space — that contains a message board where ideas can be typed simultaneously. Now, the cap is lifted. Multiple people can share at once, and more ideas can be generated in less time. This study shows how digital tools can increase participation, improve satisfaction and provide more ideas.

Let us go through some other digital tools that have made our work life even stronger.

The Cloud: Cloud computing involves access and storage of information over the internet instead of traditional local storage (on a computer's hard drive or pen drive). Today, most of our personal information is automatically synced onto the cloud. The easiest way the cloud can help you innovate is to use it as a route to market your offer and services as an application program interface (API). PayPal is a perfect example. A wide range of mobile apps and web-based businesses use it to improve sales, increase buying speed, and amplify product value.

We are often meant with the mental block when we are on a journey to solve an issue or address a challenge. Even though we may not find the final solution anywhere in sight, even taking off on such projects and innovations becomes challenging and get stuck. The key to getting inspired is to break out of routine status and find completely unique techniques and possibilities.

Some of the well-adopted external stimulants enabling you to get unstuck and make the creative juices flow by way of Digital Tools are as below. These are just a handful of examples out of multiple Apps.

Brainsparker

This is one of the creativity-oriented apps that disrupt thinking patterns and triggers new ideas to accentuate creativity. Brainsparker's random prompt cards support innovation, activate the imagination, and further ignite the best ideas. This App is currently available only on iOS-enabled devices.

Curator

App for supporting the creative process from the first bit of trigger for an idea to its presentation. This App supports the collection of data in fragmented formats like texts, objects, and images, importing from different digital media (like DropBox, Pinterest, and Instagram), and building stories to be presented. It further converts ideas into acceptable formats instantly, presents live to the audience, and distributes the presentation in pdf formats. Currently, Curator is available on iOS-enabled devices only.

Blek

A puzzle game in which users use creativity to move up levels in the game. This is a unique award-winning game about imagination and creativity. The game gets more and more complex as one moves up in the level. The game sparks thinking and different ways to address challenges. It is available on both iOS and Android platforms.

Ideament

This is a simple, paperless mind-mapping app that provides ways to quickly map out ideas. It helps in the creation of concept maps, flow charts, and outlines. This paperless mind-mapping app helps with quick idea dumps and linear thinking layouts. The App is compatible with iOS, Windows 8, and Windows phones.

Adobe XD

This is a user-experience design tool for mobile apps and web apps. Adobe XD is used for prototyping designs, creating wireframes, and screen designs for digital products. The App is developed by Adobe Inc, available on iOS and Windows platforms.

IDEO Method Cards

IDEO is recognized as one of the early adopters and proponents of Design Thinking. Offer these cards to offer inspiration and create great new designs and try new approaches. There are about 51x Idea cards divided to create great new designs and try new approaches. There are about 51x Idea cards divided into four categories: Ask, Watch, Learn, and Try. Each category defines the kind of activities involved in using each method.

Notability

We always feel that it's necessary to take notes no matter who we are. This App offers a host of note-taking and sketching tools, annotating PDF files that we record. All the details of ideas are recorded in one place. Finally, all contents can be organized without any restrictions to work further and share.

Unstuck: iOS-based App helps you through On-demand coaching, takes through peer coaching. It first helps with diagnosing what's going on really during stuck moments. The App guides one through the process of addressing new approaches to personnel and professional challenges.

Whiteboards

Let's talk about a powerful cloud tool called online whiteboard, which can be used to learn and share with collaborators. A whiteboard is simply a digital canvas where collaborators can add pre-defined templates such as project tracking and brainstorming. You can create custom templates and add images and files related to the project to have all the information in one place. All collaborators can keep up to date with the progress of the project and the shared data.

To have interactive, collaborative, and creative sessions, you can work with your colleagues on the board simultaneously and use Design Thinking tools such as sticky notes, votes, and the clock for cycles that support the creative process. The entire or partial dashboard can be exported to be presented to stakeholders.

The biggest benefit of using this digital tool with your teams and leaders is that you are creating new rituals where everybody has the psychological safety to create ideas and share them with the rest of the collaborators. Additionally, communication becomes more agile as access to the board is easy and accessible at any time.

As more and more businesses are supporting remote work, post-Covid times, employees don't need to show up at the office every day of the week. Here the digital whiteboard software has allowed teams to skip the messy email chain and go straight to brainstorming and collaboration. Some of the whiteboards are - Microsoft Whiteboard, Google Jamboard, Mural, Crayon, Conceptboard, and Draw. Chat, Realtime Board, Ziteboard.

The reader can utilize some of the suitable apps above to get creativity flourishing.

> *"The most important thing is to make technology inclusive - make the world change. Next, pay attention to those people who are 30 years old because they are the internet generation and will change the world; they are the builders of the world."*

~Jack Ma, Founder, and Executive Chairman, Alibaba Group

Master of Creativity

Remember, creativity does not wait for perfect moments; neither can it be forced.

Sometimes, we try hard to solve a problem, but we face a creative block. It may seem impossible to overcome this mental barrier.

- So take a step back.

- Relax.

- Don't rush it.

Imagine that you are standing on a beach, watching the sunset while the breeze touches your skin.

Slowly observe your mind opening up.

Creative ideas are like the rare species of birds hiding in a hole. You need to coax them out. And treat them with love and appreciation.

Using the various tools mentioned above will only help you to entice this bird out of its nest. Also, creativity is a circular process; therefore, we need to expand our scope and use an eclectic approach. Just one tool may not work for all. So, mix and match various tools to unleash creativity in individuals.

> *"In today's era of volatility, there is no other way but to re-invent. The only sustainable advantage you can have over others is agility; that's it. Because nothing else is sustainable, everything you create, somebody else will replicate."*

> **~Jeff Bezos, CEO and President, Amazon**

Fresh perspectives/Thoughts To Ponder On

Are you someone who does the same things over and over again yet expects a different outcome?

Can you think of one idea that you rejected and later regretted?

Action Plan for the Week
Creativity is a necessary prerequisite for innovation. This week, start by creating your own three if's questions that are relevant to your business.
Find a silent space, bring in a diary and pen, remove all the digital distractions, and start to doodle. While doodling, your brain will be working towards finding solutions. Make sure you are doing the activity with full awareness. This is your time for cohesive, creative thinking.
Suppose you have come out with a solution or a set of ideas. The next step is to pitch these ideas through a mind map. Put the main idea at the centre of the diagram. Now start recognizing all the means and methods. It will help you convey this central theme.
Bounce your creative ideas on to others using a digital tool. It could be Instagram, YouTube or LinkedIn. Evaluate the responses you get from the audience and work towards creating a better product or service.

Summary

Decoding the fact that creativity is not just inherited but is a cognitive process has prompted the discovery of various tools so that people can utilize them to the optimum. These tools and methods have been elaborated on in this chapter.

Foremost is the CLAD model – each of the letters of the word stands for – Convergent, Lateral, Aesthetic and Divergent.

Divergent thinking denotes the process of brainstorming to collect as many ideas as possible and then figure out the best possible solution.

On the other hand, convergent thinking implies having all the ideas stacked up before you, exploring each and then choosing the most suitable one.

Next is lateral thinking means thinking in a different way than usual. This involves originality and out-of-the-box thinking.

A in CLAD stands for 'Aesthetics'. Anything that is visually appealing gains in popularity and likeability. Therefore, emphasis on this aspect too is essential for success.

CLAD is, therefore, an effective tool for rekindling our creativity.

Studies have shown the role of psychological tools in refining our lives. Rewards and positive reinforcement result in better performance. Hence focusing on positive reinforcement (rewards, recognition & incentives help in positive outcomes).

Reaffirming the power of Meditation – is not just for relaxation and peace. Research suggests that meditation revitalizes the brain, thereby giving a fillip to creative thinking.

Mind maps – this involves thinking visually. It has been derived that when you see ideas/information in the form of images, you can comprehend it better, the task is simplified, and action is taken swiftly, thus improving productivity.

In this digital age, we cannot forget the role of digital tools and the use of apps, making our lives so much easier and processing things faster. This, too, has contributed immensely to creativity.

Chapter IV

How Creativity Sparks Innovation – Source of Exponential Growth

Just 'Creativity' (in single quotes) doesn't lead a company towards inventions and growth; innovation does!

However, innovation will not happen without creative people on board.

Let us start this chapter by understanding the basic difference between creativity and innovation.

Many a time, you will see that these two words have been used interchangeably on many occasions. There is no harm in doing that. But when we are stepping into practical application, it becomes important to distinguish both based on their specific nature.

The easiest way to understand the difference is –

Creativity is generating something novel and useful.

Whereas

Innovation is putting that something to work.

Creativity is "the capability or act of conceiving something original or unusual" (Wiley, 2013). This is the first step. The Second milestone happens when you use this creativity to become truly innovative. For example - if you are a website designer, you will start discovering unique, different market-making opportunities for your client.

"Genius is one per cent inspiration and ninety-nine per cent perspiration. I make more mistakes than anyone else I know, and sooner or later, I patent most of them."

~Thomas Edison

You will keep generating creative ideas and might even step into unusual places. However, at some point, you have to connect these dots in order to create something substantial for the future. For example, in 2014, Steve Jobs and Apple unveiled a new corporate headquarter in Cupertino, California. This new Apple headquarter maximised common pathways and workspaces, allowing people to *"connect, collaborate, walk and talk"* (Levy, 2017). Apple's Chief Design Officer worked on building a space where people are more likely to build relationships, share ideas with their teams and co-workers, and learn about opportunities to collaborate. There are many studies that suggest spending time outdoors can improve cognition and creative thinking. If you look deeper, you will understand that Apple was able to connect the dots and thus introduced Apple Park. It consisted of 6,000 trees and 5.9 million square feet of landscaping. A green courtyard in the middle of the office facility allowed employees to walk through nature as they cut across the campus.

Language is fundamental to human life. Using verbal communication, we have been able to communicate complex ideas in a simpler way, transferring them to other human beings. Animals have not evolved to that extent. Thus, creative ability is exclusive to humans. We have the ability to imagine things that are not occurring in the immediate environment. Simultaneously we also have the ability to creatively invent new words that will help us convey this information. If you are creative, you are an asset to your organisation. You can reach deep into your subconscious for that 'aha' solution. But does the story end here?

Is creative thinking enough?

Creativity involves thinking. Then comes 'producing'. Production or implementation of a creative idea happens with innovation.

Look at the example below.

Innovation comes from people meeting up in the hallways or calling each other at 10.30 in the night with a new idea or because they realize something that shoots holes in how they've been thinking about a problem.

"It's ad hoc meetings of six people called by someone who thinks that he has figured out the coolest new thing ever and who wants to know other people's opinions of his idea. And it comes from saying no to thousand things to make sure we don't get on the wrong track or try to do too much. We're always contemplating about new markets we could enter, but it's only by saying no that you can concentrate on what's really important."

~ Talk given by Steve Jobs, During Business Week 2004

From the work point of view, it is important to have creative abilities that you can use for the benefit of people or your clients. Innovation can be seen as a set of tools that aid in solving a problem or creating an advantage. These tools are not limited to humans only. Birds and monkeys use sticks to pull food out of tight locations. Hence, they are also using innovation. For us, as humans, innovation happens on a global scale.

There are three broad categories-

- *Business model innovations* - that analyse how an organisation operates and generates revenue.

- *Product innovations* - innovations that make existing material goods better or create an entirely new range of products.

- *Market innovations* - innovations that help create new markets where brands can connect with consumers more freely.

To sum it up, we can say that innovation is a demonstrable, tangible shift in a product, service or industry. Whereas creativity results from the interplay of our internal world and our external environment.

When learning is purposeful, creativity blossoms.
When creativity blossoms, thinking emanates.
When thinking emanates, knowledge is fully lit.
When knowledge is lit, economy flourishes.

~A.P.J. Abdul Kalam

Characteristics of organisations that support creativity, leading to Innovation;

- Risk-taking is an acceptable policy for the management

- Opportunity to learn from failures quickly and cheaply

- New ideas and different ways to do things are encouraged and embraced openly

- Continually challenging the status quo

- Having a portfolio of creative ideas to be successful and profitable

- Good ideas are recognised and patronised by senior management members

- Information is free-flowing rather than "necessity-proven" or demand based

- Access resources internally and enablement to access externally through participative and immersive knowledge absorptions

- A balanced attention to creativity and organisational structure, executing discipline

- Rewards for creative ideas that translate into successful innovations

- Good marketing of creative ideas through the journey from ideation to commercialisation

- Creative Leadership facilitates positive leadership in organisations to generate profitable growth through successful innovations.

"To turn really interesting ideas and fledgling technologies into a company that can continue to innovate for years requires a lot of discipline."

~Steve Jobs

How about your organisation supporting creativity and enabling successful innovations?

a. **For LEADERS** like you, here are a few quick checkpoints to assess the current levels of creativity in your organisation and positive steps that may lead to moving up to the next levels.

- Encouraging intellectual conflicts that trigger creativity within the group

- Self-awareness about their preferred style of thinking and working

- Understanding team dynamics on the style of thinking, working and preferred mode of communication.

- Sorting out and finding the sources of disagreements or differences.

b. **Your WORK Group**

- Opinions from all segments are heard, considered and respected

- Workgroups support diverse thinking that's different from the patterns of the majority.

- Leaders actively look for group members whose thinking styles differ from their own

- Help groups establish and agree upon a clear goal at the beginning of each project.

- Your group members agreed formally upon their work behaviour guidelines to collaborate and work with each other in mutual harmony and respect.

- Specifically, having someone in the team to bring in/present diverse perspectives.

c. **Your work ENVIRONMENT;** Both Psychological and Physical

- Opportunity for taking risks, associates not penalised for failures but encouraged to learn.

- People find creative assignments as opportunities to stretch their potential and take on challenges

- Openly assess risks, risk potentials, and risk management strategies (that ensures fail early, fail cheap)

- Rewards and recognition for contributing creative ideas

- Physical workplace open enough to interact easily in person across functions

- Workplace reflecting creativity stimulating objects (like arts, journals, etc., not related to business), physical orientation of tables, desks, vibrant colours, sitting arrangements, enabling open communication, etc.

- Whiteboards and flip charts placed at key spots around to scribble creative thoughts, sketches, charts, connecting dots, and an inviting environment to make creativity flourish.

For the above queries, if you find relatively higher levels of positioning of your department or enterprise, it is a clear indication of your company's healthy direction towards innovation. In case the assessment indicates that a lot many elements are missing or have very low compliance, it is time to relook at the strategic orientation of leadership towards creativity and innovative elements.

How will you bring a long-lasting change using creativity and innovation?

It all starts with society! If you can manage to plug into society and understand what it needs, you can develop products that are received as useful and elegant, thus bringing a longstanding positive change.

Creativity opens the mind, analysis the existing problems, and slowly you innovate, building research and developments to solve problems we have understood in previous chapters. But does innovation always have to be in closed rooms? Most often than not, we innovate secretly and hide the technology from others to avoid replication.

*"Innovation is seeing what everybody has seen
and thinking what nobody has thought."*

~Dr. Albert

Yet another method is –

Adopt Open Innovation Models.

An open innovation model means you allow innovations to be shared widely so that they can seed other innovations outside the original institution.

So you share information and ideas across society through a communication network while keeping an optimistic view. This model of innovation expands the market and society at large.

To adopt a truly open innovation mindset, it is important to be open to all sorts of opportunities, even if it demands time and upgrading.

Finally, creativity is a result of constant pairings or collaborations. The financial, social, and personal rewards may be great, too, as we grow along. Today there is a wide range of companies that are using open innovation in different ways.

For example, Samsung, one of the successful innovative companies today, has four types of open innovation collaborations – partnership, ventures, accelerators, and acquisitions.

Collaboration between start-up companies in Silicon Valley helps with Samsung's existing products.

Ventures mean investment in the early stages of start-ups. Such investments bring revenue and also provide access to new technologies that Samsung can learn from.

Accelerators mean providing startups with an empowering environment to create new things. The idea is that the product stemming from internal start-ups could become part of Samsung's product portfolio.

Acquisition simply denotes that you bring in a start-up that is working on innovations similar to Samsung's core products.

So, by collaborating with startups, Samsung aims to benefit from the variety of innovations that smaller companies have already come up with.

What is the present-day challenge?

Today, the challenge is to make sure that creativity sparks innovation. There are numerous creative ideas that die in the laboratory. So, it's important to follow certain clear guidelines and steps that bring transformative, innovative change.

First, a creative design has to be a 'needs-led' design. The introduction of a new product into society is often preceded by market surveys to study user needs. The user in society will make the final evaluation of whether he needs the product/ service or not!

Second, creative design can begin with discovery or development in science and technology. This is a 'seeds-led' design. Initially, basic knowledge is acquired about a new material, information technology, and so forth. Then the products are sought out to which new knowledge can be applied.

Third, have more bad innovations to have more good ones. Studies at both MIT and the University of California have proved that people who have lots of ideas, like entrepreneurs, writers, and musicians, all fail far more often than they succeed, but they fail less than those who have no ideas at all.

Fourth, sometimes our innovations act like a tortoise. Poking its head out nervously to see if the environment is safe before it fully emerges.

Thus, you need to create a tortoise enclosure - an oasis amongst the craziness of modern life. This is where marketing, strategies and other developments come into the picture. There is a whole array of work that needs to be done, from the conceptualisation of an idea to the innovation of the product.

Sparks of Creativity in Society

Society as a whole, at some point, loses touch with creativity and subdues it.

How can we promote economic growth, increase productivity, and generate jobs yet be creative and innovative in all these areas?

While innovating, you try to achieve a balance between individual pursuits and national interests.

"I run my company according to feminine principles – of caring, making intuitive decisions, not getting hung up on hierarchy, having a sense of work as being part of your life not separate from it, putting your labour where your love is, being responsible to the world in how you use your profits, recognising the bottom line should stay at the bottom."

~Anita Roddick, founder of The Body Shop

Fresh perspectives/Thoughts To Ponder On

Do you think that everything that can be invented has been invented?

Are you better at creativity or innovation?

Action Plan for the week
Make a list of all the ideas that you have turned into a manufacturable and marketable form.
Do one activity today (at home or the office) that will help you deviate from the norm and feed self-expression.
Recall your professional growth and list down all the things you are grateful for in your workplace.
Think about one activity or creative idea that has benefitted society as a whole.

Summary

Though creativity and innovation are frequently used as synonyms (another word), are these two terms the same? Technically speaking, NO. Creativity is producing something new and useful, while innovation is its application. It is the perfect amalgamation of both that ultimately leads to positive outcomes. You may continue putting in efforts without achieving anything concrete. Hence the key element is to join the dots and assimilate.

Moving to the topic of creativity in the context of organizations, factors that give an impetus to creativity are enlisted here: risk-taking, allowing employees to flex their

creative muscles and stimulate unique ideas, encouraging different ideas through rewards and recognition, failures not to be taken as set-backs but a chance to learn, improve and grow.

Leaders and senior management have a crucial role to play in facilitating creativity in organisations. A free flow of information that is not demand-based and enough openness will do the trick. Focusing on organisational behaviour techniques and psychological tools is quite effective. Team dynamics, open discussions, and even disagreements, the physical work environment, logistics, and employee interactions contribute in a big way.

If change has to take place, we need to consider the wider perspective and share ideas with the world. That's where adopting the Open Innovative Model comes into play. Spreading from organizations to sharing with the market and society should be the goal.

Chapter V

OUTSIDE the BOX is Ok, but Why do you need INSIDE the BOX Thinking?

In the previous chapter, we had a deeper immersion in creativity, sparking our Innovation Engine. What we could understand and assimilate had a common thread of the "Out-of-Box" thinking model continually lurking in our thoughts. I hope it was the same with you as a mindful explorer of creativity!

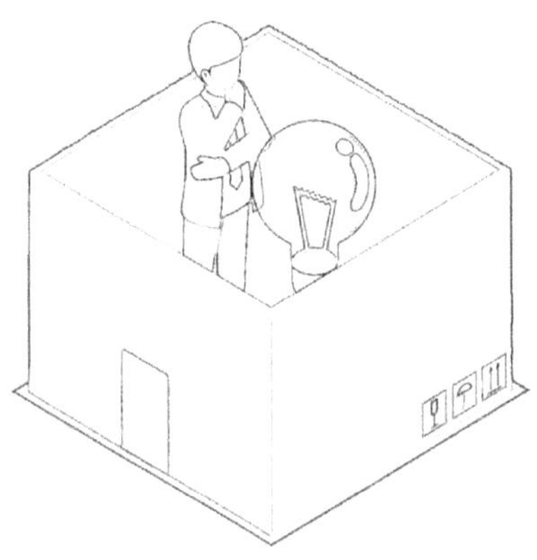

In the current chapter, you will be surprised with another completely contrasting way for creativity, compared to the stated heuristic or unstructured, free-flow of creativity abundance.

Are you constantly working or delivering creative ideas under constraints? Let's dwell upon this so-called world of constraints!

It is a general practice; most strategies are dissected, debated, and devised based on research on competitors, economic activity forecasts, quantitative analysis of existing markets and technologies, customer survey feedback, or interactions. All of the above have certain limitations for all or most, e.g., while customer feedback is highly valuable for sharing insights on current products and competitors or, to some extent, on future expectations. However, future expectations are limited to what is known to customers, who are unlikely to comment on a product that has not been experienced or is unheard of.

For e.g., the following are some of the famous market feedbacks when a new product or solution was pitched for demand! And the final outcome was absolutely contrary to pre-release market demands.

- "Ultimate demand for computers was five units."

- "People don't need Xeroxes since they would never need more than three copies, and carbon sheets can handle it."

- "Cellular phone demand is very limited."

- "Sony Walkman would be a flop."

There is a famous statement attributed to Henry Ford, a well-known innovator in the Automotive segment:

"If I had asked customers what they wanted, they would have said faster horses."

"A lot of times, people don't know what they want until you show it to them."

~Steve Jobs

The point here is not about validating the above comments but unravelling the limitations of market feedback.

Most companies encourage wild thinking to get "out-side-box" or "out-of-box" creativities to enable product improvements along with analysis of available quantitative market research data sets.

Although an "Out-of-box" or "no constraints" based environment is to enable and nurture creativity, practically, there can't be timeless or infinite resources to get creativity out apart from the limitations of such a method as described above.

Constraints

In the current economic environment, it is generally acknowledged the fact that everybody works under many constraints all the time and explores alternatives, permutations and combinations to create solutions or address issues on hand within the confined space and time. However, imposing too many restrictions may also curtail creativity. For e.g., if you assign a team or individuals to come up with a new idea for

a new business in 15 minutes, people either give up or no ideas crop up due to lack of effort limited by extreme challenges like this one.

In this chapter, constraints being defined as not two extremities of wild, open and unlimited resources and also not too many stringent restrictions. Create a new box with certain boundaries to look at very closely, issues and resources just around; that's the "Inside-Box" approach we are referring to. In the current chapter, we work around creativity within our "closed world" by deploying different tools.

What is a **"Closed World"**: By definition, *"When solving a problem or creating a new solution, try to use only the resources that exist within a product, service or system itself or its immediate vicinity"* (Credit to Dr. Roni Horowitz). This will force us to rely on the resources at our immediate disposal and not to go wild around, creating constraints leading to creative solutions. The closed world consists of current components, the relationship between the components, and the current concepts.

Cognitive Biases: We have a tendency to overlook the creative ideas and solutions that are just around to pick them and arrange them due to these biases. Let's understand these cognitive barriers.

Functional fixedness: In the 1930s, a famous German psychologist demonstrated the phenomena of functional fixedness through an experiment. (Candle experiment). The outcome demonstrated that once a certain function is associated with an object and is performing that function, it is impossible to imagine additional functions or tasks that the object can perform. E.g., When the Titanic ship met with an accident with a huge iceberg, many passengers and crew on board drowned in the sea, and few could use lifeboats. The Iceberg was overlooked for its function as a temporary shelter to save lives by keeping people afloat, but just as a cause for the accident, same with plastic chairs on-board.

What causes functional fixedness is our neurological tactic that screens out awareness about features that are not important at the first instance for use.

Structural fixedness: We look at an object as a whole with a defined structure and with a mindset that it cannot be divided or rearranged. E.g., Control buttons for television are always expected to be on the bottom side, and any other position is perceived with discomfort. Another example, we always expect passage between driver and co-passenger in a car to be in a certain way only. Or we believe that the engine of the passenger car is always on the front side.

When handed a product and asked to create a new design or variation on it, people tend to fixate on the features of the current design. Structural fixedness needs to be broken to have creative outcome outcomes or solutions. Structural fixedness is another barrier to creativity.

"Systematic Inventive Thinking"(SIT) Method: New creativity Tools (Templates) and details shared here are conceived by Prof. Jacob Goldenberg and the team over two

decades and expanded to cover a wide range of innovation-related phenomena in multiple contexts. I understand from publications that these ideas were inspired by pioneering researcher Gingrich Altschuller, who discovered underlying patterns in highly innovative products. I found these SIT tools useful when applied to certain projects during assignments. These tools support systematically breaking this fixedness and being open to creativity around the functions or structures or objects.

Using these tools doesn't require extraordinary talents for creativity. Simple to use, low-cost, step-by-step approach to spark innovation.

Function Follows Form: Psychologists Ronald A Finke, Thomas Ward, and Steven Smith reported the phenomena of "Function Follows Form" in 1992. They recognized two kinds of different approaches towards creativity, that is, Problem to solution or Solution to the problem. They discovered that people are good at connecting solutions to addressing problems. With certain configurations available, people tend to connect where all these configurations may be applied directly or with certain changes.

Above is the opposite of striving hard to find creative solutions to a well-defined problem on hand. (This is usually "Form Follows Functions")

In the approach of "Function Follows Form", we start with an abstract, concept-level solution using templates and connect to the problems that the solution can address. In using the principle of SIT (Systematic Inventive Thinking) method, we follow the "Function Follows Form" approach.

E.g., If we ask you to take 20 Kg of weight up the hill, you will start thinking of multiple approaches to solve this challenge. Instead, I handed over a backpack and asked what we could do while climbing, which can be related to one of the above-mentioned challenges. Another example is; Mercury thermometer used for measuring temperature by raising the mercury levels in a tube as the temperature rises.

Though we claim creativity is heuristic, and one may wonder about mentioning the following templates, consider these templates as enabling tools to make creativity simpler!

These following five templates offer excellent navigational support to creativity and innovations considering *"closed world"* premises

Subtraction Template: You could take away an important component from a system, product or service; thereby, you can see new opportunities.

The process is simple. You identify the most important components of the product or process you are working on and mentally force them out. Usually, a component without which the product or process doesn't function! Then, think about what all configurations the new product or system can address. However, this looks crazy, but it helps in creative solutions that can solve many problems.

A Few examples of the above pattern or templates applied are:

- Taking out balancing small wheels on the rear side of bicycles to support balancing practice for riders

- A famous airline removing the seat allotment process itself, which ensured an open system where passengers could arrive in time to secure their seat of choice.

- Installations of ATMs for cash dispensation, no physical banks! And staff for cash administration at ATMs

- Open universities, mortar and brick structures of formal education replaced with the distant, online education system, incredibly enhancing reach to learners by depth and breadth.

- ATM (Automatic Teller Machine) dispenser supporting cash withdrawal without ATM card (Using mobile banking for Authorizations and dispensing cash)

- Famous shampoo company manufacturing water-free shampoos and offering solid shampoo cakes that can be used with water. This saves liquid handling complications, supporting transportation, storage, and handling logistics.

- Driverless passenger cars or autonomous driving.

Subtraction with Replacement: In this method, it is not just subtraction; there is a replacement component from within the closed world that doesn't perform its original function. New products or processes are reviewed for potential applications, customers, market, viability and so on.

Process

- List out all the major components

- Identify a component and visualize how the product or process loses its original functionality without that component. Component elimination may be full or partial.

- Visualize all issues the new version of the product or process is likely to address.

- Evaluate the feasibility of resulting in the REALITY of a new configuration; can we create a new product, service or opportunities for refinements?

Division Template

We learned just a while ago about the limitations of Structural fixedness on creativity. By using a division template, challenges of structural fixedness are addressed, thereby paving the way for new realities. Structural fixedness perceives physical objects as if they exist as a whole and cannot be modified or rearranged further.

The Division template is executed for its functional fixedness, too, when applying the tool to a Product, service or system as a whole. The existing system is divided into various components further rearranged into time and space.

This will potentially create a new configuration resulting in a new product, system, or process or offer offers new benefits to users. With this, we go beyond what we initially thought could only be feasible. By dividing into components, one gets multiple degrees of freedom, enabling higher levels of creativity relatively.

Some of the samples of successful products, services, or systems that can be related are:

- Moving control buttons of television sets to a remote-control unit

- Airline check-in over the web (web check-in), moving the passenger check-in process away from the airport

- Patient blood sample collection away from the laboratory to home collection, assisting millions of patients and improving medical services.

- Online movie ticket booking, avoiding long queues.

- Internet banking services allowing account holders to carry out money transactions at any time, eliminating the need to visit banks in person.

- Refrigerators moving the freezer unit to different locations instead of the traditional top only or bottom only. Even going beyond that to have a centralized compressor, enabling users to decide which cabinet to be a freezer and which for normal cooling, thus offering a multitude of possibilities.

- Movie theatres offering the best eatery experiences while watching movies and dining was relocated.

- Another excellent example of a Time-based Division template application is IKEA furniture being assembled at the user's home rather than at IKEA plants

- Pharmaceutical formulations where ready-to-consume medicine is prepared at home by the user by mixing powder and water (or other liquid), purchased as separate units/kit.

Process

- List out major individual components of the product or the most important steps of a chosen service

- Describe each component or each services step in the current configuration

- Rearrange or reconfigure those components or steps within a closed world

- Visualize all possible configurations and their usefulness in a new configuration

- Pick what suits most as innovative, its uses, potential users and market, and further viabilities for commercialization.

Multiplication Template

Pick up a component, copy it and its change attributes, then use it in a counterintuitive way, may be a strange way! The change in the attribute is not only quantitative but also qualitative.

Let's understand some of the examples to get to know more:

The twin-blade razor set is a classic example of the multiplication principle being applied, one blade to pick and hold hairs so that it doesn't stick back to the skin, the other one to shave, thereby ensuring a close shave. One blade is copied one more time but set at a different angle to serve the purpose.

Imagine a fast-moving consumer goods segment in which food items are packed in multilayer packages with different

textures, finishes, and materials to ensure edible items retain their originality and freshness. Each layer of primary packaging is an example of multiplication with different attributes.

In a multicolour ballpoint pen, each colour refill is a copy of a coloured pen, where attributes are changed to offer multiple colours like red, blue, black, and green.

Yes, you are correct! Here we are breaking structural fixedness, which confines an object to its format and cannot be envisaged in any other structure or format. So, further, to recap, "Function Follows Form" is an approach in which you do not look for a problem to be solved and start cracking towards a solution but rather the other way around; by having a conceptual solution out of the current set of products and systems, by re-configuring physically or by the system.

Process

- List out major individual components of the product or the most important steps of a chosen service

- Describe each component or each services step in the current configuration

- Pick up a major component or process element that stands out, copy it (make multiple copies), change the features (attributes) of each copy to a completely different one, and put back the changed element(s) into the product or process.

- Visualize all possible usefulness in a new configuration. Who? Where? How? Questions

- Pick what suits most as innovative, its uses, potential users and market, and further viabilities for commercialization. Also, it could potentially solve an existing problem that was not thought to be solvable in a direct way so far.

As I am referencing this template, I just recall my childhood days; my home had two clocks, one in the living room and another in the entrance area. The first clock in the living room was set as per the standard time. My father used to be very strict about his expectations, timeliness and preparation for his daily needs before proceeding to work (A much-disciplined manufacturing set-up back then, where I, too, gained my early career tractions). Also, on his return from work, to alert my mother or children to keep things ready, the clock at the entrance used to be about 15-20 minutes ahead so that things were well in control.

Task Unification Template

Imagine bicycles of the early days; in addition to maintaining traction, the rear or front wheel of a bicycle used to act as a prime mover for a miniature dynamo attached to it to generate electricity to light-up small lamp set-up on the front side. During the night, the rider would press the attachment to the wheel to activate the dynamo. The wheel was performing additional tasks beyond its primary task.

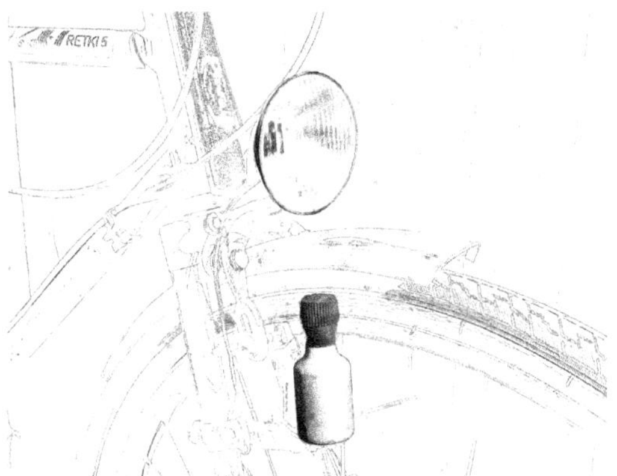

Another example is a door handle incorporated with a numeric lock on the handle, functioning as a lock in addition to a basic handle function to open and close the door.

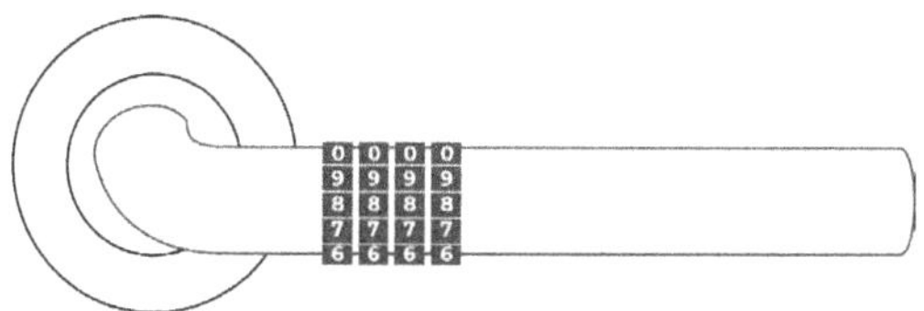

Imagine you are entering a clinical area or hospital room by pushing the handle on the door. Now, let's attach a sanitiser droplet dispensing action to this door whenever the handle is pushed open. Thus, a new task has been attached to the door handle in addition to the current function

Every time a key on the computer keyboard is pressed, electricity is generated by the piezoelectric effect. Keys generate electricity in addition to their normal functions whenever used, charging an internal battery unit to have an extended period of availability.

You are travelling in an urban transport (bus or train), and the sides of the bus and interiors carry advertisements about products/ services for sale or some other topic, apart from transporting people and goods.

A famous radio channel communicates strongly while airing music is also mixed with an ad in a creative way. Sometimes, consistent communications that are not heard attentively on a plane get meshed up with well-known music tunes or songs.

In the above cases, we see the breaking of functional fixedness, leading to creativity and further innovations.

Process

- Identify a component or process step that is performed currently

- Identify new tasks that the selected component or process step can perform. The component should now perform the new task in addition to its original function

- Repeat the above for multiple components, getting a new set of tasks in addition to the current one

- Choose your favourite, most useful combination to work on further identifying users, customers, markets, etc.

Attribute Dependency Template

Let's explore nature and our daily routine a bit to understand the attribute dependency tool.

- Think about a chameleon. Its body colour changes according to the colour of the tree branch around it. Body colour is an internal element or component, and a tree branch is an external component or environment or element.

- You are in a hurry to get to work, so you rush to a nearby café and buy a cup of coffee. The lid of the coffee cup changes according to the temperature of the coffee. In this example, the temperature is an internal element of the coffee cup; while the lid is an external element that changes colour.

- During a hot season in one geographical area, hotel management sets different tariffs to attract travellers to stay there. The season is an external element to the hotel, and tariff is one of the main components of the hotel.

- A daily used toothbrush; the colour of the bristles changes upon certain no. of uses

- During the local festive season or peak seasons, a hotelier charges a higher rate than usual.

When we observe the patterns in the above examples, we can clearly see changes in internal components or elements with alterations in external components within the closed world.

One of the variables is getting changed due to modifications in another component, and this is called dependency. Changes in the external component in the closed world cause a change in the internal component of a product or object.

In the "Attribute Dependency" template, we start exploring establishing new relationships between internal components and external components within a closed world that doesn't exist at present. Or we break the relationship or dependency that already exists between the internal component and external component.

Process Steps

- List out all major variables (not all the components) within the product, services, or system.

- Identify major variables that are associated with this product or service, or system within the immediate environment or what we say as a "closed world."

- List these variables in rows and columns in a matrix form, mark with "1" for already existing relationships or "0" if there is no relationship between those variables.

- Next step, wherever there is no relationship, we try to establish a new relationship among variables and visualize a new version of the product or services that may realize into innovative solutions or a new set of offerings to users.

- Identify potential benefits, users, markets, etc

- An example is shown below for a ready-to-wear shirt manufacturing company.

- Let's list out variables in the shirt to start with

- List out external variables connected to the closed world of "shirt."

- Plot these variables in rows and columns

Shirt Attribtes	Shoulder	Collar	Chest	Full Sleeve Length	Arm Length	Shirt Length	Waist	Fabric	Side cut	Short sleeve
Shoulder	1									
Collar		1								
Chest			1							
Full Sleeve Length				1						
Arm Length					1					
Shirt Length						1				
Waist							1			
Temperature										
Casual wear										
Formal wear										

The above table shows a sample for basic measurements, and another shown below offers extended variables that can be established as other basic internal variables along with other external variables (Though they are not in exact template format, a listing of variables, the reader to explore further).

Variables	Size of shirt	Color of Shirt	Collar shape	Half sleeved	Full sleeved	Cotton Fabric	Other Fabrics	Formal shirt	Casual shirt	Price of shirt
Winter Season										
Summer Season										
Rainy Season										
Liesure time										
Office time										
Economical										
Affordable										
Emerging market										
Mature market										
Student										
On-the-job class										

Summary

At the other end of the spectrum of 'Outside the box' thinking is 'Inside the Box Thinking', which is the focus of this chapter. In this approach, there are 'constraints' imposed on creative thinking. Though the word 'constraint' has a slight twist in this context and denotes neither totally open with no barriers to resources nor having too many restrictions, but somewhere in between. These constraints can be related to time, i.e., expected to complete a task within a certain time frame or limited customer feedback to proceed on the path of creative pursuits.

How can creativity develop within a so-called "closed world" is further elucidated. "Closed world" means utilizing assets/ resources available within a product, service or system or close vicinity only.

It has also been observed that we are liable to avoid ideas or solutions found just around us, in our close surroundings. Known as 'cognitive barriers', this is seen as a setback for our creative juices to surface. These blockages are primarily related to our neurological patterns and the way we think-

- **Functional Fixedness** – not seeing beyond the regular function of an object

- **Structural Fixedness** – believing any object cannot be in any other form than what we are used to.

To counter this issue, there is the concept of 'Systematic Inventive Thinking', consisting of tools that support systematically breaking this fixedness and being open to experimentation. Following a step-by-step approach, which is-

- **Function follows form** – start with an abstract, concept-level solution and then connect it to the problem.

- **Subtraction Template** – refers to removing the most important component from a system, product, or service, compelling us to come out with new suggestions.

- **Subtraction with Replacement** – a step ahead of the previous point; removing and replacing.

- **Division Template** – wherein the existing systems are divided into different components and rearranged or modified.

- **Multiplication Template** – choose a component, copy the same and then use it in a unique way by changing its features.

- **Task Unification Template** – adding tasks to the existing ones

- **Attribute Dependency Template** – exploring and establishing new relationships between the internal and external components.

We can derive from the above analysis that creativity isn't just a magical gift bestowed to only a few lucky individuals; it is a skill that is easy to develop and master.

"RID" Formula to Navigate through Disruptive Times

For the last few years, global economic activities have seen big shifts on many dimensions, would like to bring forth a few of them in the following contexts. The trends witnessed intense value-creating opportunities and high competitiveness, societal challenges as well growing ecological challenges. Most recent challenges out of the unprecedented once-in-a-century pandemic of COVID-19, supply chain disruptions, and destructive war among borders in Europe, energy crisis.

Some of the key highlights those bringing large disruptions:

- Rise of India, China and other eastern countries into global economic activities

- The rapid spread of digital technologies

- Economic and social disturbances due to the COVID pandemic

- Supply chain disturbances due to lack of material and skilled, necessary manpower

- Swift technological evolutions in Digital technologies space, specifically Industrial Automation, Internet of Things, data science, Artificial Intelligence

- The emergence of new and innovative players to the fore, driving revolutions in industry space

- Smartphones enabled with the internet are changing the way we live, communicate, interact and transact economic and other needs

- Shifting focus of economic activity to India, China, large capital, people and information flow

- Emerging economies offer better shareholder values and returns than matured markets

- Emerging economies offering global competitiveness for technology and services

- Global value chains are evolving at a rapid pace with localization, automation, decoupling large dependencies, and localized production closer to the consumer place.

- A shift in demographics, an increasing aged population in the key matured market and an increase in the non-working population (retired from the workforce), few economies are taking advantage of the young-age working population

- The accelerated pace of technological progress creating significant opportunities for enhanced value creation, redefining workplace engagement patterns.

- Uneven adoption of technological developments across segments, companies and countries

- Large scale Digital identity drives covering huge populace as an enabler for social and governmental benefit transfers (e.g., India initiative of AADHAAR, unique digital identity)

- Some economies, regions and segments are winning handsomely at a very large scale on one side and on the other side, equally opposite, deep downslide on account of not being able to make the best use of emerging scenarios. This is leading to highly skewed contours of large growth, gains and large economic losses. Ripple effects cause social discontent and disparities, too, leading to high protectiveness.

- Demand for energy savings, racing towards carbon-neutrality or net zero targets, sustenance initiatives towards bringing positive social impacts, clients, vendors, employees and investor attention towards SEG initiatives.

- The pace and frequency of business transformation needs have shortened intensely over the years

The above scenario calls for a pragmatic look within organizations in assessing the situation and a strong need for a well-crafted strategy akin to survival instincts for the present and creating a wished-to-be future, thriving even during disruptions.

The recommendation to navigate through these disruptions is to apply the **RID** (Reinvention-Innovation-Design Thinking) formula in a structured way that is scalable and deployable in a strategic way.

Entrepreneurs have multiple degrees of freedom to choose RID with a strong base of creativity in business.

One may choose Reinvention (since ideally, 100% of the population has this capability) as a fundamental mindset aided by an "Innovation" approach and highly customer-focus solution offerings with Design Thinking processes. There are high probabilities of a successful and exciting journey encompassing these key elements with "creativity" as the core.

The reinvention cycle encompasses a continued transformation from healthy chaos to stagnation or stability just only until a new trigger for a new set of reinvention journeys begins.

Each of the elements of RID is covered in the following sections.

PART II

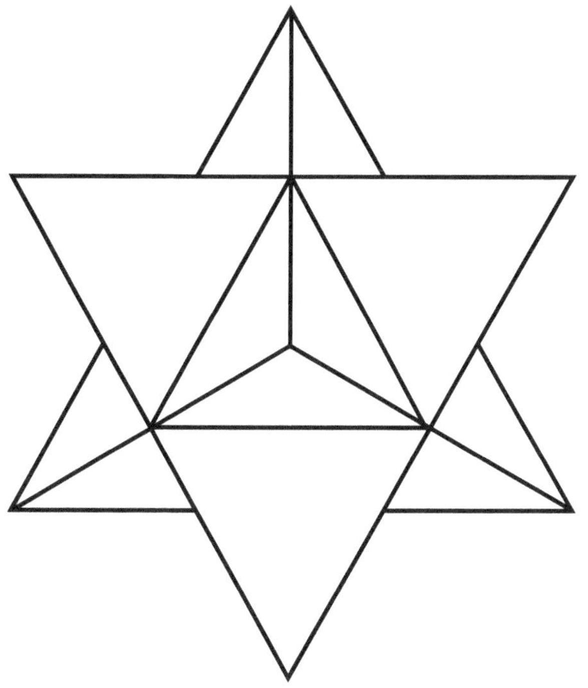

Reinvention – On a Mission to Transform Your Business

Disillusionment and uncertainty had settled in the business world as the world was gripped by a pandemic in 2020, as a nationwide lockdown was announced in India. Shops, malls, offices, and factories were all closed indefinitely.

A to Z, the manufacturers of a popular brand of shirts, found themselves in the midst of all this chaos, closing their production unit with a heavy heart and asking all employees to stay at home. What else could they possibly do? Management had not planned for such an eventuality; their store had been closed indefinitely. Quite a few businesses are like this; we rarely anticipate such events or are too arrogant/ overconfident to believe that such an event could occur. The pandemic was a wake-up call.

That's when the textile company's leaders and management put on their thinking caps and started brainstorming ideas. They had sufficient time now to come up with ways of staying afloat. Of course, nothing could be done while the lockdown was in effect, but once it was lifted, they needed to redesign and implement their new strategy - the first step toward reinvention.

Anticipating the spread of the virus, they were aware that things might not come back to normalcy quickly. Even after a few months of easing out of the lockdown, people may not venture out for shopping. Moreover, who would buy garments if most people had to stay at home and work from home? Sometimes partial lockdown could be imposed, and caution had to be administered in every sphere.

The mask had become a necessary item and was mandatory. No one could go outside without them. Masks were popular all of a sudden, becoming part of the attire. Cloth masks, in particular, gained popularity because they were more comfortable, washable, reusable, and available in beautiful patterns and designs (Mentioning about approach, not the medical efficacy of these masks)

As part of their survival strategy, the idea of manufacturing cloth masks instead of shirts dawned on A to Z. With the plan in place, it was simple to put the plan into action, design, and implement the change of producing a substitute product. Further, in order to reduce marketing time and money and also for customer convenience, the masks were sold in apartment complexes personally by their team members. The venture was a success due to the high demand for fabric masks.

The point over here is about embracing the new reality to stay afloat, and there could be many alternate ways to brave the storm and sustain business beyond surviving for the moment.

Introduction to Reinvention – Concepts and Unique Learning from Nature

As we remember our Biology lessons, the extraordinary transformation of caterpillars into butterflies through metamorphosis is unforgettable. Metamorphosis is a process of transformation from one thing into another. During the spring season, we witness nature at its finest, with birds making nests and caterpillars turning into vibrant butterflies.

Source: www.freepik.com

Nature provides ample opportunities for all living beings to change throughout their lifetime from one characteristic form to another. This transformation process is evident in all aspects of life and is also applicable in the business world. It shows that nature supports the improvement of living at different stages through the process of reinventing oneself to adapt to new realities.

By definition, Reinvention has the following varied meanings:

- According to the dictionary, it's a noun and "is an action or process by which something is changed so much that it appears completely new."

- It's "the act of producing something new based on something that already exists, or the new thing that is produced."

- As a verb, it means to "give something a different form or purpose."

- It is "a systematic approach to thriving in the chaos that includes ongoing anticipation, design, and implementation of the change via continuous sense-making, anticipatory and emergent learning, and synthesis of cross-boundary, cross-disciplinary, and cross-functional knowledge."

- It means a structured and deliberate effort to engage in healthy cycles of planned renewal, building on the past to ensure current and future viability.

While hit with the worst-ever waves of the pandemic due to COVID-19, we kept hearing questions like — When will this pandemic end? When are we going to get back to normalcy or business as usual? What else can be done? Will my business

survive, or my job is there? As a management or business owner, how do I cut costs? Do I get back to my social engagements?

These concerns had become quite normal at many business encounters and within families expecting stability. Most of us believe that those days are over! The volatility or VUCA (Volatility, Uncertainty, Complexity, & Ambiguity) world is here to stay.

This recent pandemic has also brought in many fundamental shifts in lifestyles, business interactions, outlook toward life, human societal engagements, and so on.

The pandemic took away the employment of countless individuals and tragically took the lives of numerous loved ones. Its effects will continue to be felt for years to come. However, our business economy has faced similar crises numerous times in the past. An alternative perspective: whether it was the great recessions of the 1990s and 2000s or the current pandemic, only a few businesses survived, a few flourished, and many more failed. Is there a deeper meaning to be learned from this?

Multiple studies and data points provide profound and meaningful insights:

- Numerous enterprises have survived beyond 75 years. Though over the decades, the number of such long-existing organizations has reduced drastically.

- The life expectancy of successful businesses has declined over the years ranging from 75 years (e.g., Fortune

500, about 50 years ago) to 50 and 30. And now, in recent years, the average surviving rate of companies continues to decline to about 15 years.

- Hordes of organizations have thrived on longevity with once-in-a-lifetime disturbance or need for change, milking and deeply exploiting the status with little or no change.

- This very change was like a one-time project rather than an ongoing adaptation.

- Organizations had the luxury of abundant time to get out of disturbances or change requirements. An essential factor was to brave it out to pass through challenges, survival instincts, or a few measures as a project.

This leads to an important question about ways and means to continue thriving, not just staying afloat in the midst of disturbances.

As we explore ways to overcome such challenges, let's understand what makes businesses sink or get into an irrecoverable mode, leading to bankruptcy or insolvency.

Business Cycle — S Curves

A business cycle is represented through successive stages of start-up, growth, scale-up, and mature stages, typically in the shape of "S" or sigmoid. This represents the business growth pace over time. The period of such a cycle depends on various factors around the business. From start-up onwards, the business experiences rapid growth at some point, scaling up before it flattens off.

The longevity of sustained S curves represents the resilience and flexibility of organizations in the business world. However, the key element is how successfully the business navigated through critical inflexion points.

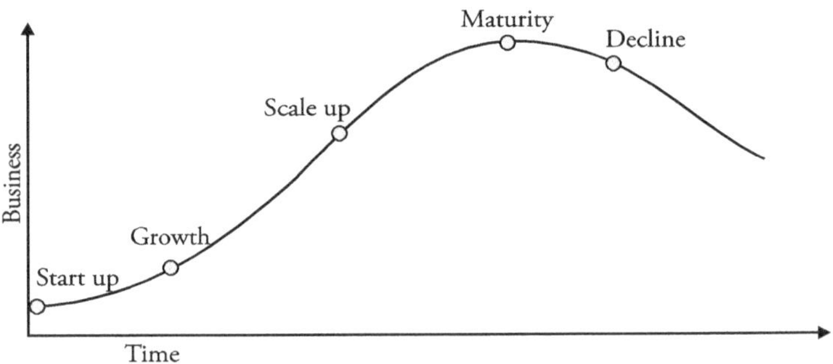

As businesses scale up and enter a growth phase, a set of processes and cultures become entrenched, making it challenging to alter or adjust these processes. At some point, a sense of pride (and sometimes an arrogance stemming from past successes) can set in, leading to a lack of sensitivity towards changes in the business environment, such as new competition, evolving technology, changing customer expectations, and emerging talent expectations.

An attitude of "invincibility" or "too big to fail" due to strong business performance up until a stage of maturity may go unnoticed, and the most difficult period of decline may already be underway. However formidable the organization may be, there will eventually come a time when it has reached its limit for growth.

Chief reinvention officer Dr. NadyaZhexembayeva terms it "Titanic Syndrome", which makes an organization sink. It's essential to identify such a syndrome well ahead of time to keep companies stay afloat and navigate ahead.

Dr. Nadya describes Titanic syndrome as "a corporate disease in which organizations facing disruptions bring about their own downfall through arrogance, excessive attachment to past success, or inability to recognize the new and emerging reality."

If we actively redirect our focus from simply surviving to continuously learning and evolving, we can not only survive but thrive even in chaotic times by constantly reinventing ourselves and our businesses. Evolution is no longer a one-time project but rather a continuous, systematic process that requires the right mindset, processes, and systems in place.

If I ask you a question or you ask your manager or businessman about what is their key challenge, the immediate answer is, "how do I keep afloat" during these challenging moments?

Fast-paced economic shifts, technological evolutions in the field of IIoT (Industrial Internet of Things), Digitalization, E-commerce, Artificial Intelligence, geopolitical conflicts (like war), supply chain disruptions, new post-pandemic (COVID-19) norms, substitute products, reduced time-to-market for innovative products, changes in lifestyles, are constantly bombarding business establishments, struggling to stay afloat and move towards growth (Sustain and thrive).

How and When to start reinvention?

With the business life cycle rapidly declining, enterprises must constantly evolve in order to sustain growth. This is achieved by a series of sustained S curves that reinvent themselves periodically or definitely at *inflexion points* throughout the journey.

What separates performers from staying on the top over a sustained period is how one successfully transitions from the maturity stage of the cycle to the growth stage in a quick next cycle and on an ongoing basis.

When competitors start moving ahead in some of the critical areas at a faster pace, your current products are no longer differentiated one, Failure to adopt fast-evolving technologies, competition acquiring your customers, and finally, a clear talent gap indicates an immediate need to navigate the inflexion point to have sustained growth. The need is to prepare ahead, to respond with a planned action for a strategic inflexion point instead of a panic response. The usual approach of *"If it isn't broke, don't fix it"* doesn't work here, but to fix ahead with the right decisions.

Inflexion points are natural appearances on a growth journey, like a ship on a successful journey encountering multiple icebergs. Such icebergs cannot be avoided but can be prepared to be navigated. Strategic inflexion points are opportunities for growth, and considering them, the market is demanding a shift in your strategy to stay afloat and grow.

The inability to recognize such icebergs may lead to organizational disasters leading to a severe decline in revenue, market share, takeovers, and, finally, bankruptcy.

How to recognize icebergs or hurdles?

Recognizing these demands of understanding such icebergs and planning a way to address them has increased the need for REINVENTION

Let's glance through a few successful enterprises that fell through or got into a deep decline for some well-known reasons. Some of these could continue but at a different scale, offering varied perspectives on stalled growth or failures.

Nature and its inspirations

While we continue to discuss the life span of enterprises, businesses, and their journey of transformation towards a better side or decline, let's shift the gears towards nature for a while

Introduction to Biomimicry

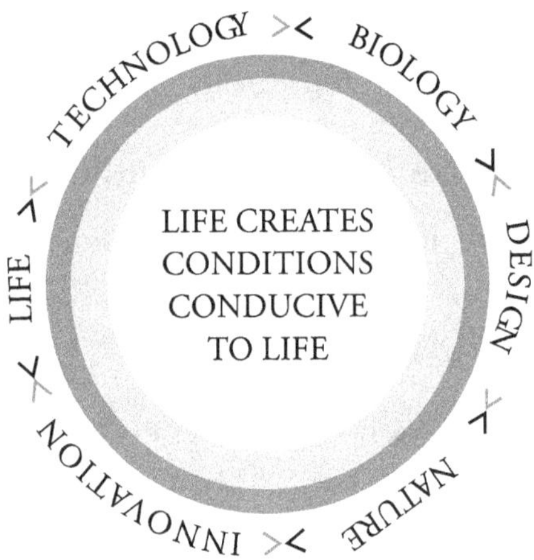

Biomimicry is an interdisciplinary approach and a conscious emulation of nature's genius. It connects the disconnected worlds of nature and technology, biology and innovation, and life and design. This practice of Biomimicry seeks time-tested wisdom of life to design a table that has sustainable, practical solutions, borrowing life's blueprints. Biomimicry at its best connects humans with nature in the best way possible, aligning and integrating by understanding natural earth processes.

I am pleased to share information about essential elements courtesy of the Biomimicry3.8 institute.

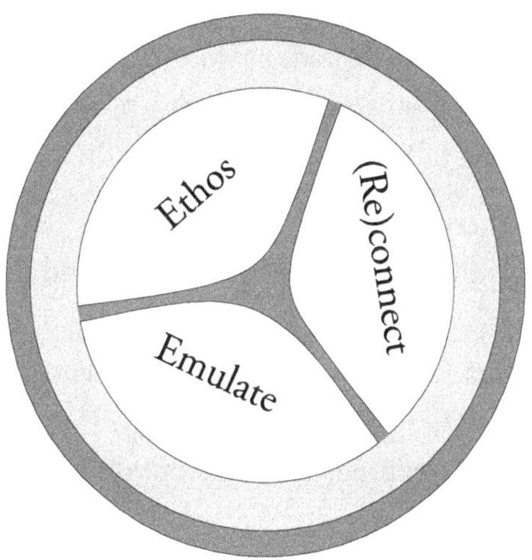

The practice of Biomimicry embodies three interconnected but unique ingredients; the Three Essential Elements of Biomimicry represent the foundation of the Biomimicry meme. By combining the essential elements, bio-inspired design becomes Biomimicry.

- The **ethos** element forms the essence of our ethics, our intentions, and our underlying philosophy for why we practice Biomimicry. Ethos represents our respect for, responsibility to, and gratitude for our fellow species and our home.

- The **(re)connect** element reinforces the understanding that, while seemingly "separate," people and nature are actually deeply intertwined. We are nature. (Re)connecting is a practice and a mindset that explores and deepens this relationship between humans and the rest of nature.

- The **emulate** element brings the principles, patterns, strategies, and functions found in nature to inform design. Emulation is about being proactive in achieving the vision of humans fitting in sustainably on the earth.

Here, the term "Design" or "Designer" is meant to be anyone responsible for conceiving, creating, and implementing ideas that affect human, cultural, technological, social, scientific, or financial systems at any scale. Perhaps you didn't realize you were designing, but when you create some new form that had not existed, that makes you a designer.

LIFE's Principles

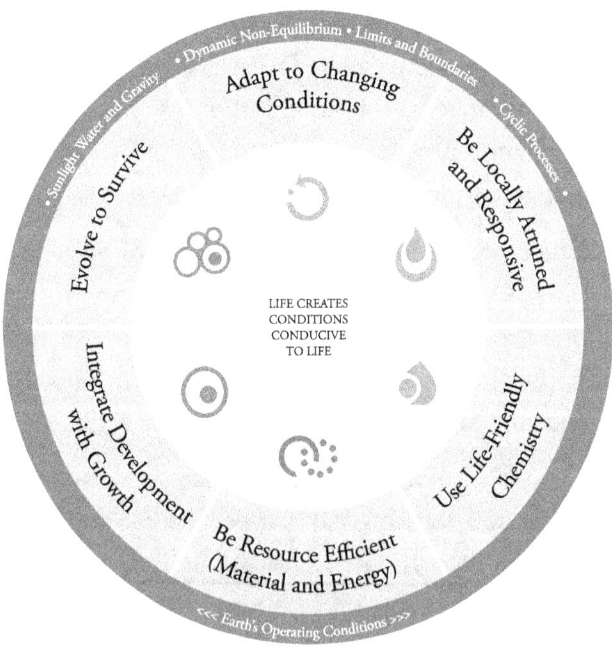

Life's Principles represent these overarching patterns found amongst the species surviving and thriving on Earth. Life integrates and optimizes these strategies to create conditions conducive to life. By learning from these deep design lessons, we can model innovative strategies, measure our designs against these sustainable benchmarks, and allow ourselves to be mentored by nature's genius using Life's Principles as our aspirational ideals.

What can be learned from nature, which has been around for over 3.8 billion years? How can life in a system be protected, nurtured, and elevated to higher levels?

- Making sense of the system
- Scanning
- Strategic surveillance
- Anticipating change
- Assessing and Measuring, designing change
- Implement/execute change
- Understanding the processes that sustain life
- Adapt to changing conditions
- Leadership and communication (Meerkat mammals as an example)
- Teamwork and flight efficiency (Gees following V-shape to enhance flight efficiency) and leadership transitions
- Constantly connected to ground realities (stay grounded)

- Agility and Constantly evolving to survive (Ants, bumble bees)

- Integrate human development along with growth, not just business economics

- Creating a condition conducive to life

Meerkats constantly scan the environment for any threats, and the leader keeps communicating with the team while others collect food. Ants store the food for the rainy season by anticipation. Geese flight in V format to enhance flight efficiency and also leadership transition on the fly, as well attention to needy & tired ones. The above natural phenomena and actions of lives around clearly indicate how strongly reinvention happens in the environment.

REINVENTION is a process that encompasses "Anticipating change, Designing Change, and Implementing Change" as key pillars supported by a reinvention mindset, reinvention culture, and a system to support the whole of the Reinvention journey on an ongoing basis.

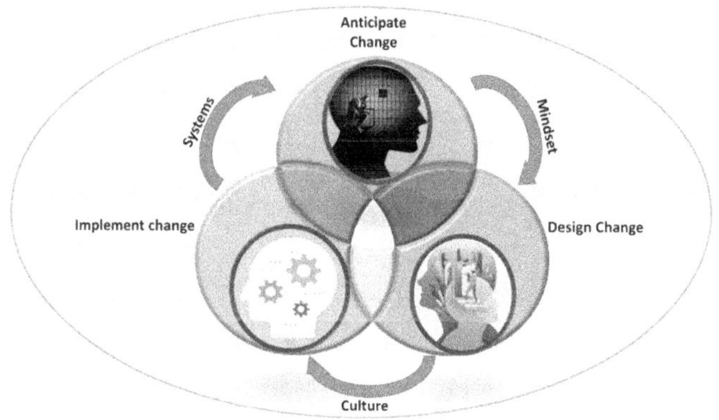

Chapter II

How and when to Reinvent – Strategic Levers for Being UNSTOPPABLE

Let's get back to the S curves of the business cycle, refer to the image shown below. If there is an intervention by way of reinvention at the ascending slope of the S curve, the chances of business continuity and growth are more than 90% in contrast to having reinvention carried at the descending side of the S curve. At this stage, the chances of getting back to growth modes are less than 10%.

So, it is not just about reinvention happening but ahead of time to ensure a smooth jump happens to the next series of S curves for sustained growth.

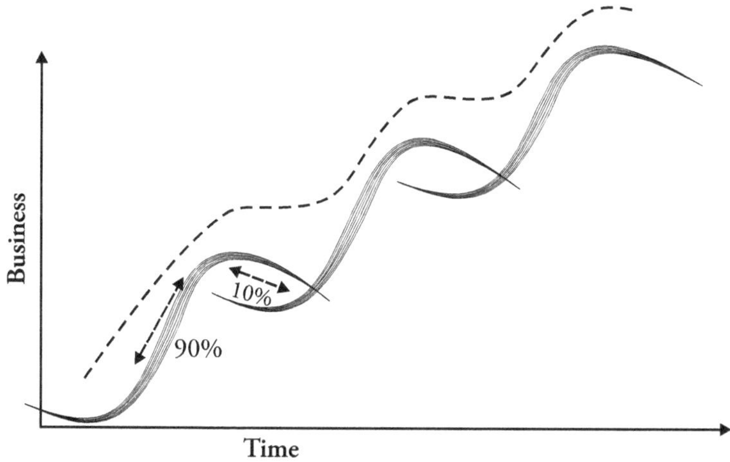

In one of the surveys conducted (source: www. Chiefreinventionofficer.com), we found from the feedback that 60% of managers felt the need for reinvention every 2-3 years, and another 28% felt the need for reinvention every 4-5 years. It's pretty clear that the frequency of reinvention had a significant impact on the survival and thriving of organizations.

For most enterprises in need of addressing reinvention needs, stages appear as strategic inflexion points or stall points. These stages are also termed turning points or downturn points. These are the points where management needs serious intervention leading to REINVENTION.

How to navigate through the need for REINVENTION?
In the previous section, we understood about main reasons attributed to organizations; let's take the next leap into navigation.

Understanding our standing

When market disruptions hit a company, and the company is in decline, panic reactions usually flow quickly, getting into survival mode and overcoming immediate challenges, focusing on the here-and-now scenario.

Organizations make the mistake of doing too little too late on incremental steps to navigate the winds and tides, despite the pressing need for a significant or radical change at the system level.

Following quick checks come in handy in making an assessment of our standing in the disruptive winds or living with *Titanic Syndromes* organizationally.

a. Get to Know or Anticipate:

- What are your sources of signals for market disruptions and feedback? Is it the same set of sources like customers, suppliers, consultants, or research teams?

- Employees are rarely or very less engaged in sharing market insights.

- Do market warnings stay within small groups or setups?

- Belief in an "Ever Green" Talent pool, despite the inadequacy of the TALENT Pool

- The falsehood of Market Dominance or declining dominance

- Belief in Perpetual Patents of Technology or products and services

- Ignorance of new market entrants and irrelevance of Technological differentiation

- Company in a REACTIVE mode most of the time than PROACTIVE on potential market threats?

- Critical CUSTOMER FEEDBACKs take backstage

- Not enough time was specified to work on Creativity, Innovation, Strategy, and reflection

b. Design or formulating CHANGE approach:

- The company is proud of the past and strongly favours continuance to pass through disruption

- Highly frustrating to start NEW or CHANGE, even its for the BETTER

- Strong arguments on why new things or ways may not work

- Deflection of FAILURE attributes to market, competition, vendors, Government policies

- NEW products, solutions, and concepts are, MOST OF THE TIME, a push-down approach

c. IMPLEMENT or Execute change:

- Rarely handled or exposed to start and execute change management

- Visible, Distinct gaps between Commitments and intent to EXECUTE change

- Limited commitments of RESOURCES and Absence of SYSTEMS

- Ineffective or inefficient executions, very big SAY-to-DO ratios!

- High INTERTIA within organizations to respond to market needs

- Low motivation and rare celebrations of successes

If the response to the above diagnostics is an affirmative YES, most of the time, it's a clear diagnosis of the need for REINVENTION. The scale and intensity of the syndrome may vary in the above three elements indicating the challenges at different stages of the need for CHANGE management

Relating the above challenges to our discussions on S-curves of the business cycle; would offer deeper insights into navigating the REINVENTION process.

Since strategic inflexion points occur at any point of S-curves, the anticipation of those events well ahead makes organizations prepare well for a smooth transition to the next set of growth curves.

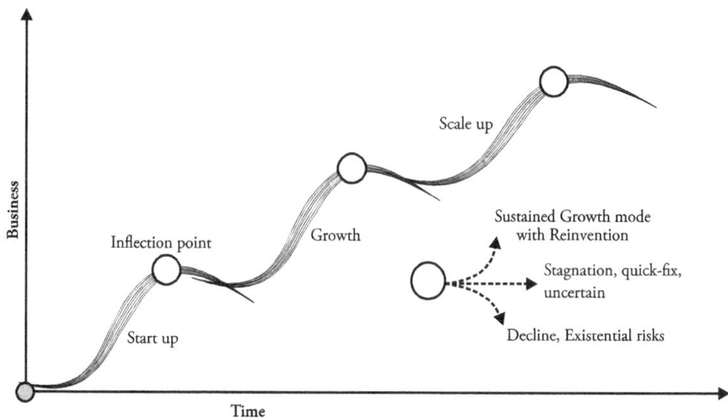

Though inflexion points shown above are depicted as happening at the rising edge of different stages of the S curve, such events may happen at any time. Also, inflexion points vary depending on many internal and external factors (Process, economic policies, talent, competition, company promoter's interest, etc.). The impact of Reinvention depends entirely on how organizations respond.

Even with a lot of effort, a company finally decides to go for reinvention despite soaring profits, happy shareholders, satisfied employees, and handsome market share; will be met with low chances of successful transformation. In a research by Mark Bertolini, and David Duncan, published in an article (HBR-2015), about 80% of executives recognize the strong need for transformation but only about one-third are confident about getting it done successfully over 5 to 10 years.

While the timing of reinvention has the highest rate of success during the growth stage, making it too early may result

in not enough yields out of investments and efforts already made. Hence it is desirable to have a small set of incremental reinventions on an ongoing basis and radical or major reinvention actions ahead of inflexion points.

Strategic Levers for Reinvention

Consider the "Strategic Levers" framework to understand when and how to REINVENT. These strategic levers are the ones that made the business successful and potentially could become a source of the decline, too, unless diagnosed with evolving status. These strategic levers are major undercurrents shaping the longevity of S- curves and points of inflexion.

1. **Competition:** As business starts growing, the set of competition in the segments starts increasing with new entrants, and non-competitors start becoming competitors, enhancing the fight for food. Market and differentiation exploited can no longer exist to keep growing. Failure to respond quickly may lead to a decline in business growth and eventual declines. The emergence of stronger competition, mergers, and acquisitions among market players strengthening their ability to play, may curtail business growth trends. The cell phone industry, for example, has seen several changes for both manufacturers and service providers. High performers see changes in customer needs and become leaders in the creation of a new set of competitive differentiators for the industry while continuing to exploit current businesses.

Quick checks: Following quick checks enable businesses to respond suitably-

i.   Entry of new competitors in the current market

ii. Non-competitors becoming competitors (new players altogether)

iii. Market entry strategies used

iv. Significant Changes in go-to-market models

v.   Entry into your customer strongholds, even though appears to be with insignificant values

vi. Changes in value-proposition offered in terms of products and services

2. **Industry Position:** The kind of niche enjoyed while starting the business may not remain the same with the emergence of new technologies, new players like non-competitors becoming competitors, customers becoming competitors or vendors turning into competitors. Technological or value propositions offered as a differentiation may no longer continue to be a differentiator. The emergence of the digital marketplace and the convenience of customer touchpoints may alter customer buying behaviours. Xerox was highly dominating in the copier and printer market; with the emergence of other Asian players, business was impacted largely, even on repair and services with low-priced local solutions. Xerox quickly remodelled its offering not only as a copier and printer company but extended as a full-line corporate business

services company, reinventing itself at the visibility of early signs and many big corporate customers outsourcing these services.

Quick checks: Following quick checks enable businesses to respond suitably-

- Do you see a consolidation of major players with mergers and acquisitions?

- Are there any emerging technological disruptions on the horizon

- Are customers building capabilities within to optimize cost and perceived efficiency aspects?

- Are there any other external forces diminishing your role in the industry?

- Weakened entry barriers or changes in customer usage or consumption patterns of products and services?

3. **Success factors alignment:** We may call it success factors or organizational performance indicators (KPIs); traditionally, it will have revenue, cash flow, sector growths, profitability, debts and credits, and so forth. These parameters show business successes on current and probably a short-term horizons too. However, it may not guarantee nor assure future trends and may not reflect market confidence, customer loyalty, etc., as a sign of the continuance of growth trends. For example, Adobe started looking at the number of subscriptions

(annual, renewals) received and corresponding revenues instead of revenue measurements dominated by the number of software packages/licenses sold. This subscription model offered a multitude of benefits to customers beyond the great experience of document creation and reading. Some of the organizations also showcase no. of new customers acquired during the accounting period.

Business corporates may not publish these KPIs publicly, but I have experienced some of the leading business enterprises religiously working on elements that are of great importance beyond the usual balance sheets and key highlights.

Quick checks: The following quick checks enable businesses to respond suitably-

- Do our offerings reflect what the customer is looking for as futuristic?

- Does "Value creation" out of offerings means the same as customer perception and experiences?

- Are we capturing customer satisfaction as a success factor? Like Net Promoter scores, customer loyalty indcx, purchase experiences, etc.?

- Do we see a correlation between the Customer Satisfaction Index and our revenue and profitability? Are our revenues as strong as the customer loyalty Index?

– Do we have a group of customers who are loyal to us because of our value proposition? Will they migrate if a new supplier appears? Is the current situation the result of a lack of alternatives?

4. **Customer Needs:** When we as a supplier analyze a set of top contributing customers and a bottom few set of customers on various parameters, it would reveal interesting attributes for customer retention while also triggering potential risks in those accounts. Depending on the business model, the depth of understanding of final consumer or end user customers' needs varies and sometimes loses real needs unless user experience or user needs are known. Recall the successful R&D team intervention in understanding real customer needs or "Job to be done" when P&G contemplated a new razor for men's shaving focusing on India's geography. A deep, immersive customer empathy journey was carried out by P&G executives. It's a great example, and the product became a really successful one.

Another classic example of addressing customer needs was the just enough entry-level car, "Nano", from the house of TATA to transition bike users to a car at an affordable price. While the approach was good, resulting in an example of "Reverse Innovation", the product did not succeed greatly to the expected levels for various reasons. The intent, approach, and supply chain ecosystem working towards achieving conceived product was a great example.

A miniature, portable ECG machine innovation by GE targeting specific geography, considering power quality and transportation needs, and potentially addressing the health care of a large populace is a great example of keeping customer needs in focus, covering both latent and explicit specific needs. The key success factor was to make it available at an affordable price to work under challenging, harsh environments.

Many organizations, while planning to introduce a new generation of product lines (again on the lines of S-curve), carry out the extensive voice of customers (VOC) even before finalizing specifications of the product being conceived by reaching out to various customer segments (user, intermediary, supply chain partners, consultants, etc.) to capture feedback on current product lines and future market expectations, competitive play etc.

Quick checks: Following quick checks enable businesses to respond suitably-

- Do we carry a set of customers who carry the baggage of unmet needs?

- Customers continue still and may switch over if a potential new vendor appears to addressunmet needs. Competitors may potentially acquire these customers

- Do emerging technologies being pursued eventually help in addressing unmet needs?

- Is there any mismatch in the requirements of B-to-B customers and end customers of these products and solutions?

5. **Business Models:** We have been experiencing and also studied; over the years, business models have evolved significantly. The advent of the Internet brought about numerous technological, economic, and social revolutions in how we interact and conduct business with customers and vendors. A simple example is the transition from brick-and-mortar to by-click online booking of airline tickets and hotel reservations. The customer-supplier ecosystem had transformed from product-based to system and then platform-based solutions bringing a whole set of experiences and business eco-systems. Industries have moved into a variety of supply chain solutions to serve their customers and so forth, bringing wider transparency and traceability.

Technological shifts and regulatory needs (to some extent) to transform the automotive segment on account of fossil fuel (Petrol or Diesel engine based) to Electric Vehicles are constantly changing the way a final vehicle is delivered. Major implications and needs are being addressed by considering the REMOVAL of some items, ADDITION of functions, REDUCTION in some aspects, and INCREASES in some experiences being delivered. This has led to realignments and shifts in the automotive vendor-manufacturer ecosystem.

This EV (Electric Vehicle) transformation topic triggered a huge transformation in the automotive industry, shaking up the whole supply chain of automotive components and manufacturing needs, and every participating vendor is forced to REINVENT. This is one of the major disruptions offering a gigantic opportunity to Reinvent, stay afloat and keep growing.

Many capital equipments which are not regularly used get served through various commercial terms (like Pay per use, lease, partnership, or shared basis) too. Some of the services get into operative expenses mode instead of being offered as capital expenses. Cloud services are used as new platforms and subscription models for software instead of buying/licensing one.

"Just because the current business model had worked successfully long, doesn't guarantee it will survive and thrive in future too". Netflix offering content streaming was a great example of business model innovation despite challenges and existing strong support for rival DVD mail order services as subscriptions

Quick checks: Following quick checks enable businesses to respond suitably-

- Any immediate or emerging competition embracing new business models?

- Customer journey resilience and customer experiences at various stages? Are there any weak links in processes?

- Do existing business models survive through strategic questions applied to emerging technologies, changes in customer buying behaviour, market trends in similar market segments, the way profitability is computed, the continuance of market differentiation, etc.?

- Are there any new, profitable and sustainable business models being applied in other segments?

6. **Talents and Capabilities:** Despite extensive revolutions in Artificial Intelligence, Data Science, and Digital Technologies, nothing can replace competent human resources in organizations. It is one of the best practices to continually assess what kind of organizational structures, skill sets, and expertise are needed to address current market needs but also futuristic ones.

The absence of requisite skill sets and competencies reflects in most of the above Strategic levers for enterprises and factoring human resources aspects makes it easy to address disruptions. For example, the whole of the global economy is experiencing an unprecedented "Great Resignations" saga over multiple geographies, not sparing any of the economies, whether matured or emerging or transitioning. The economy in the United States of America is already experiencing great resignations at this stage while this book is being authored. World Economic Forum predicts that more than 40% of executives resigning from their current jobs during 2022 and 2023. This will cause huge disruptions and already demands an urgent intervention by way of Reinvention of human resource engagements.

An indication of unpreparedness or not being configured for the future with existing resources or new resources expected onboard can be a huge cause of concern for a potential strategic inflexion point. Early recognition of future competency needs and creating an environment for constant Learning and Development is necessary. This will also include assessing future needs, learning and development (L&D) spending, L&D infrastructure, content management, L&D delivery approach, alignment with strategy and business functions, systems for assessment of impacts of L&D initiatives, etc. This also needs to look at organizational set-up or Organizational Design (OD) initiatives to address imminent disruptions. Talent attraction, Retention, and Development strategies being formulated and executed on an ongoing basis ensure the healthiness of organizations from a human resource perspective.

A recent survey depicted growing organizations with top performance had very focused, future-ready L&D initiatives in place, not just for today but for thriving tomorrow too. In order to enable transitions to a new set of S-curves, successful organizations build distinctive capabilities ahead.

Quick checks: Following quick checks enable businesses to respond suitably-

- Do we possess skill sets to serve the future needs of customers and other internal stakeholders?

- Alignment of strategy and business units on talent needs

- A strong team of leaders to embrace transformation in technology and delivery methods

- The company is able to attract new talents that suit the future and also ability to retain talents, re-skill, retrain, and redeployment methods in-place

- Performance appraisals linked with competency development and deployments

- Managers reviewing and owning talent management and retention is not just an HR function but across-line functions.

- Learning and Development (L&D) teams and strategy in place which is constantly monitored and supported with sufficient budgets?

Reinvention is a constant cycle running across the organization involving the "Leadership Team" to trigger Reinvention and thus leading the Change and the "Management team" to manage the complexity of change and make Reinvention successes.

It's a continuous cycle of "Healthy Chaos to stability or stagnation". Within an organization, many functions or the whole of the organization will be at some point on this cycle of constant transition from Healthy Chaos (Multiple orders) to Stability and vice-versa. There is a likelihood, that there could be multiple Reinvention cycles and transformation efforts within the organization. These transformation efforts need to be recognized and supported.

To make Reinvention a success, it needs unwavering attention and contribution from leadership teams and management teams.

Chapter III

Organisation set-up – Don't Bow to Challenges, Empower the Culture

Top Executive setup

Some executives are great at constantly managing the financial S curve for enterprise; some will be better at managing growth trends for manufacturing, geographical expansions, product management, extensions, and creating new markets. What is needed is a system that aligns the capability S curve of the organization with business growth aspirations. What is needed is a top executive setup that not just manages the financial S curve but also focuses on building distinct capabilities to thrive tomorrow.

As a concern with REINVENTION being a strongly pursued initiative instead of a once-in-a-while activity, it is recommended to have focused resources and organizational structure. Some of the options could be as below-

Option-A: A dedicated resource or lead heading this function outside the mainstream organization but may be as

a legal entity to execute with significant independence or as a separate task force.

Option-B: A dedicated resource within the organization as a dedicated function driven by an experienced Reinvention expert or equivalent, anchoring across multiple segments and functions.

Option-C: Reinvention efforts are embedded across all functions and driven within all functions to keep evolving and performing, considering the needs of today and tomorrow for thriving. These functions might drive their own performance metrics, budgeting etc.

Any of the above options would fit the organization based on need, timing, size and change management culture, business goals, etc.

Establishing REINVENTION system:

1. So far, we could understand the concepts of S-curves of business growth, transitioning to continual growth curve, and understanding strategic levers of Reinvention shaping S-curves.

2. Let's explore our approach to establishing Reinvention systems in an enterprise.

3. Basic elements of the Reinvention system have three basic elements starting Anticipating Change, secondly Designing Change and finally, implementing change. To execute all these three cycles, we need a Reinvention mindset, Reinvention Culture and Reinvention ready

Systems. Having three basic elements addressing the immediate needs of Reinvention is necessary; At the same time, it is necessary to establish cohesive, collaborative, cross-functional systems to achieve the organisational goals of the ongoing Reinvention process.

By simple process, elaborative answers and curative activities for diagnostics questions raised in previous steps on *Titanic syndrome* fit well for executing Reinvention cycles.

1. Anticipating Change

This process is about keeping your ears to the ground or well connected to gather deeper insights about emerging shifts in the industry, economy, technology etc., beyond our regular sources. Establishing a system to gather information from a varied and new set of sources is one of the many ways. Having such a trend-watching mechanism will support in identifying imminent threats from competition in the near future.

This structured approach of getting insights, e.g., threats, help the company in getting converted into a business opportunity well ahead. Having dedicated cross-functional teams and appraising teams to act upon on a regular basis in an easy understandable manner with actionable data is the core of action in anticipating change.

Many growth-oriented organizations do this activity, with the exception that chances of approaching the same set of sources are the big change to be embraced. Getting insights from non-customers, views on competitor actions, ground-shifting technological disruptions, a new set of supply chain participants, a new set of consultants, etc., are some examples.

Animals at Anticipation stage: *Each Meerkat mob will have a sentry (normally called Matriarch, a single dominant female Meerkat leads) to lead, watch over the mob, keep watching, make sense of any danger and warn other members about the threat. The sentry watches from the top of a tree, top of a bush or rock and looks around. When other team members work on foraging the food; such a cooperative system in nature is amazing.*

2. Designing Change

The process of Design, per se, is to create or transform into something new from the current form or afresh. The Design processes go through opportunity identification, prioritizing, customer empathy journey, prioritization, solution development and iterative prototyping, and finally, commercial viability. In the Reinvention process, we tend to carry the best of core, shred off everything else and create something new. Designing change doesn't mean we let go of everything but carrying the best learning and what is relevant to the new anticipated scenario. The company is expected to retain the core and make the best use of it in a new form to fit new dynamics. Some of the approaches to designing a change could be Design Thinking, User Experience, Appreciate Enquiry, Creativity & Innovation, etc.; the catch is making these relevant, impactful and participative across the organization.

Nature inspiring a Design Change

Exteriors of buildings with rough surfaces are subjected to more dirt and dust, making it difficult to clean and maintain them afresh. The structure of lotus flower leaves inspired a German company to develop and design a new paint system that fends off dirt naturally with its new micro-rough finish surface, like lotus flower leaves. The hydrophobic structure of the leaves of the lotus plant minimizes the contact area for dirt and water.

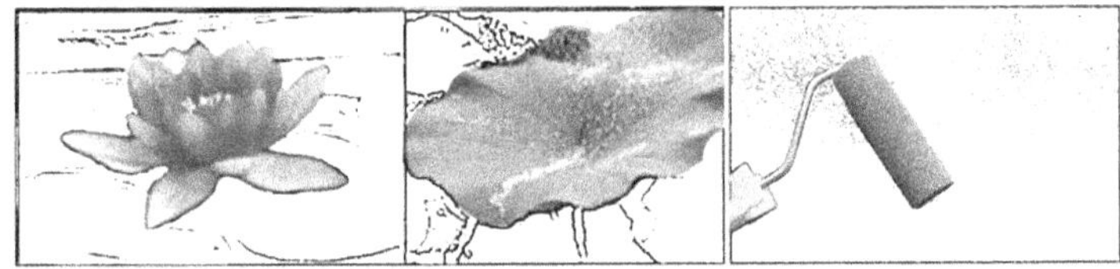

3. Implementing Change

This is all about the implementation of the changes we designed, navigating the finish line of success, and initiating the next set of reinvention cycles. This process is about achieving our milestones, celebrating even a small success, learning from failures, and calibrating the journey as new challenges and opportunities emerge during execution. This implementation stage offers the opportunity to put in place some of the important tools, such as Emergent Strategy (instead of linear strategy where needed), effective change management, and collaboration across functions. The Implementation step also involves establishing a rhythm for the reinvention cycle, building new capabilities, and strong, motivated teams, and offering optimum resources (including budgeting, competency building, and talent development for future needs)

"To improve is to change; to be perfect is to change often."

~Winston Churchill

Implementing change encompasses identifying lead measures connected with goals, commitments cadence among teams, the cadence of reviewing scorecards (achievements) and course corrections where needed with clear intent to achieve goals of Reinvention.

Successful Reinvention is an intersection of triggering and anticipating change proactively, as well as a thoughtful design that is future-oriented while continuing to reap strong benefits today through strong collaboration, participation, and appreciation for efforts; finally, adoptive, agile but navigating through potential resistances.

Nature demonstrates quietly how life on earth adjusts to the cycle of change in seasons, lives transforming to suit to changing environment, acquiring new skills, cooperating with the ecosystem, protecting their territories, protecting and growing off-springs, enhancing the level of life, cementing interdependency. At the same time, trees shed their leaves in autumn, new greenery during spring, and are strongly rooted, surviving and striving during winds.

Chapter IV

How to Strengthen
the Reinvention Systems

In order to have a continued successful Reinvention cycle, an infrastructure or strong foundational elements are needed.

"Culture eats strategy for breakfast" – Peter Drucker, Legendary Management consultant. It was meant to emphasize that an empowering and powerful culture is a necessity to make strategies successful.

Strong foundational and protective elements of the Reinvention system are the Reinvention mindset, Reinvention culture, and Reinvention ready systems.

Reinvention Mindset: Generally, mindset is a set of our beliefs that shape how we make sense of the world and self; this influences how we think, respond, feel and behave in a situation most of the time. A reinvention mindset is a set of beliefs in the nature of change as a need to survive and thrive not only today but for tomorrow. Individuals and organizations that believe in shedding old beliefs, values, and systems that are no longer supportive of new environments but also create opportunities even during adversity. These shifts in the mindset start with reframing some of the strongly stuck beliefs into a new belief system to support today.

Some of the examples of a supportive Reinvention mindset shifting from stuck beliefs that no longer work;

General Survival Mindset	Reinvention Mindset
Change happens once in a while. Let's brace through	Change is constant. Prepare ahead to survive today and thrive tomorrow
Fix issues just enough needed for today	Fix issues for the day and build for tomorrow's success
We are too big or too great to fail and sink	We are too big, still, prepare for "Black swan" moments
We hold a dominant position with no chance to fail	We hold a dominant position but continue to prepare for new competition likely to enter
There are patents that shall survive unchallenged	There are patents that may not be lost for long; let's reinvent
Avoid challenges, attribute to external sources	Embrace challenges, and convert them into opportunities
We have been successful with this system, no need for a change	Open to a new system to be successful while carrying best practices and grow further
If it ain't broke, don't fix it	Break it before someone else does
Run one time, an isolated project to change demands	Establish a deliberate system for proactive measures

Reinvention Culture: Cultureis a reflection of collective beliefs or mindset in organizations that are deeply rooted and shows up in multiple arenas of business. The work environment that offers an opportunity to experiment and fail, to fail early and cheap, how to celebrate successes and how failures are responded to represents a Reinvention setup. The rituals we carry when high on performance and responses during downtime reflect the culture of an organization. The Collective mindset to let go of past successes, ability & willingness to embrace challenges, proactively working on potential icebergs of disruptions, and navigating to succeed not just today but also thrive during chaos represents the Reinvention culture settling in an enterprise.

Some samples of rituals that define the Reinvention culture are shared hereunder:

- Celebrate and recognize even small successes that drive and motivate employees

- Do not celebrate failures. Celebrate learning, E.g., An organization conducting a celebration of learning from failures and awarding a "Golden Egg" as a reward for best sharing out of creative failures. One of the largest Indian conglomerates, the TATA group, reportedly experimented "Dare to try" initiative inviting teams to share their stories that weren't successful; it offered a great learning opportunity

- A system to capture competitive movements on a monthly basis among dedicated teams

- A ritual of informal meetings with senior executives of distribution companies to get to know market dynamics

- A ritual like "No-agenda" connect with a team of selective employees and offers a platform to reorient and develop as evangelists for Reinvention in different pockets.

- Breakfast or lunch meetings with select talents to seed the Reinvention plants, the potential for successful propagation of a new mindset, and finally getting converted into a new Reinvention culture.

A new culture is established with the ability to unlearn, learn, re-skill, appreciate, and reframe beliefs that are no longer supportive, appreciate enquiry or curiosity mindset, future orientation, embracing change with a set of rituals and converting them into habits.

Reinvention-ready systems: While it is great to have committed leadership to trigger the cycle of Reinvention to sustained growth even in the backdrop of disruptions and a management team to manage through the healthy chaos triggered by Reinvention; A highly essential one is to have an efficient and effective system in place to support the Reinvention execution as a key enabler. With clear intentions to navigate uncertainty and a host of disruptions, it is necessary to have flexible, agile systems in key functions like finance, operations, logistics, Human Resources, and Information technology infrastructure, and tools to monitor a set of KPIs reflecting the Reinvention journey. For e.g., a finance system where budgeting is flexible enough to adjust to real needs, a system to assess where to invest, or go for small breaks.

Initiatives rolled out as part of Reinvention are measured for both lead measures (which are controllable before an event occurs) and Lag measures (post-event outcomes, no longer controllable) that contribute towards success factors. (One such example is Business Dash Board as Power BI tools),

Learning Index aligned with Future talent needs, Set of customer satisfaction Indices.

A system to navigate "Emergent strategy" execution reflecting progress on the journey with multiple disruptions versus "Deliberate Strategy" designed for a calm ocean journey in stable, predictable market dynamics.

Amazing but true

225 Years of Illustrious journey of Rexroth organization reveals how the organization REINVENTED itself over such a long period since the year 1795. The organization not just survived the turbulence but continues to prosper, getting future-ready with its continued Reinvention. For any Reinvention practitioner or student, studying the journey of Rexroth as an organization offers a sense of fulfilling learning.

After a long journey, Rexroth has moved from a Water-Driven forge to a leading Digital-Hi-Tech company much ahead of its contemporaries for the portfolio.

It was in the year 1795; Georg Ludwig Rexroth started a water energy-driven forge in the Spessart Mountains in Germany and one of the oldest tech companies transformed into a thriving Hi-Tech pioneer in the industry, imbibing all the advancements in Technology but with its strengthened core. The below image depicts the great transformation journey that Rexroth had successfully passed through over the years.

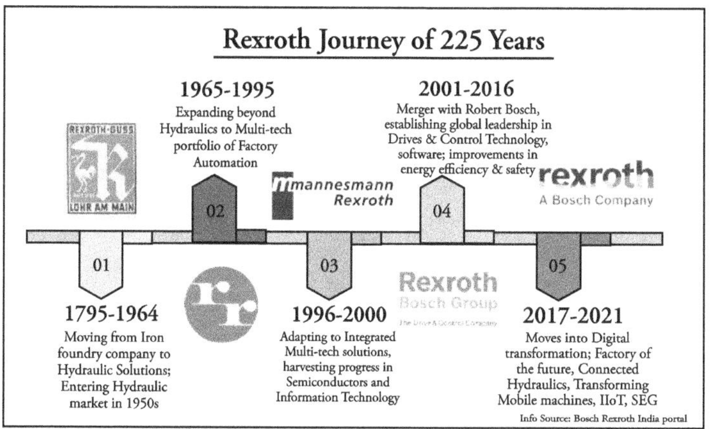

"Over the past 225 years, Bosch Rexroth has seized the opportunities offered by technological advances, turned them into innovations, and adapted its business model to them," In the pride comments from Rolf Najork, Executive board member of Robert Bosch GmbH with responsible for the Industrial Technology division, and CEO of Bosch Rexroth AG.

The simple process cycle for Reinvention

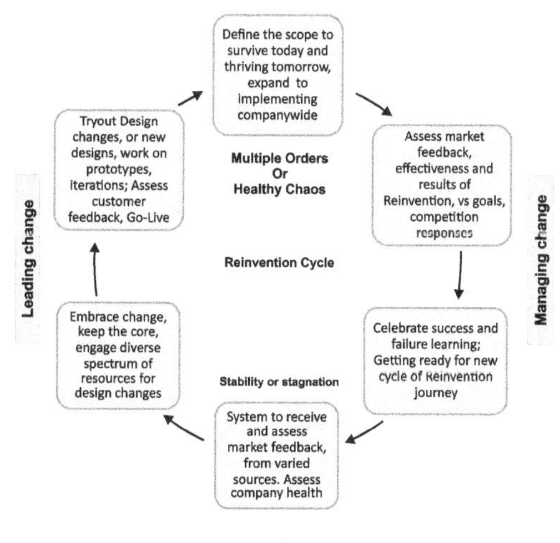

What to go for; Innovation or Reinvention?

As we come to the final lap of the Reinvention topic, let's clear the air about the potential questions about whether to go for an Innovation.

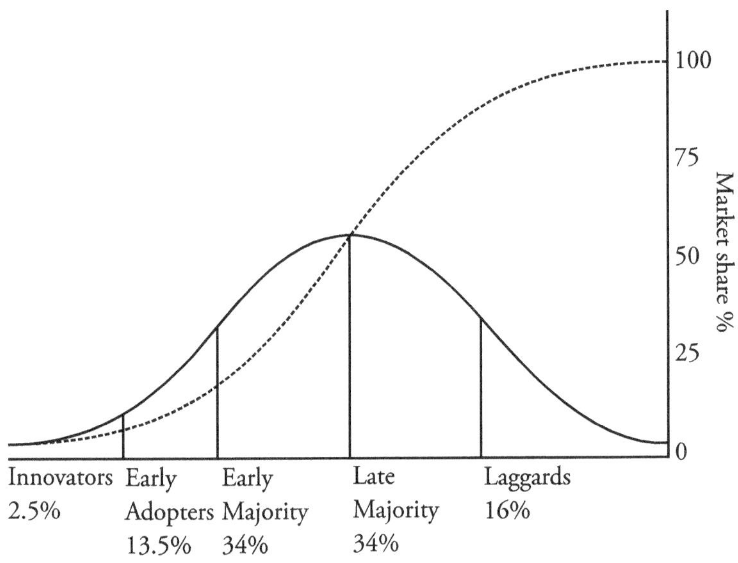

What suits you and how?

The law of Diffusion of innovation, according to Everett Rogers, presented in 1962, shows different segments of consumers in a given market. According to this theory on diffusion of innovation; only about 2.5% of consumers out of the whole set of markets are innovators! As a corollary, it means about 97.5% of consumers are non-innovators. Those inventions get tested by about 13.5% of consumers who have the most liking for trying new things.

These early adopters propagate the message and influence 34% of mainstream consumers for innovations. Further, 34% are late adopters following the innovations; look around for how it works and how it feels to be part of innovation consumption. Finally, the last segment is laggards of 16% who resist every change unless they are left with no options or driven badly to the wall to adopt those innovations. (For example, continue to use fixed landline telephony as long as services are continued and use postal services for written communications; though which appears to be more exaggerated).

The above theories lead to an interesting inference and are true too by Dr. Nadya in her famous book; namely, that while only 2.5% of the population can truly innovate, the remaining 97.5% plus these 2.5% innovators can Reinvent in one or more forms. Every individual has inherent Reinventing capabilities and needs to pursue these native capabilities to strive and thrive.

Everyone can be useful in bridging the "Now, Next and Beyond" system by imagining small, incremental, affordable changes in simple ways to make things better for life.

Contours of Creativity, Invention, Innovation and Reinvention-

- Creativity is applying imagination to solve a problem or challenge,

- The invention is creating something that didn't exist before

- Innovation is a useful application of Invention or combining existing ideas in a new and useful way, offering a significant change to users.

Reinvention comprises all of the above competencies applied depending upon the need and stage of S-curves of business growth. Some organizations may become just incremental innovators or radical innovators either at the growth stage or just around strategic inflexion points.

Quick Thoughts: As an experienced reader with the above inputs, what is your opinion on the following questions?

- When was the last time your organization experienced Reinvention?

- Recent reinvention was it an incremental change or Radical transformation?

- What was reinvented most recently? A product, an entire solution or a whole ecosystem connected with your industry?

- How frequently has your organization reinvented to survive and sustain growth?

- Do you get a sense of Titanic syndrome when you connect with your leadership or managers?

- Does the industry eco-system where you perform subjected to a strong VUCA scenario leading to panic responses?

- How does your immediate competition respond to customer needs and change demands?

- Do you feel an urgent need to kick-start reinvention, or can you sustain for some more years as is?

- Do you feel your career or job is secured? Any risks due to market situations?

- How do your daily personnel routines fit into new norms post-COVID-19?

- Do you feel your learning curve is in the right direction to keep fit and enriched to take on new responsibilities?

- Are you confident to take on new tasks with evolving technological changes and market behaviours?

Record your responses that come to your mind at first for addressing Reinvention needs in your department or function or private life too.

Summary

The solution for most of the problems businesses are facing in a VUCA world (volatility, uncertainty, complexity, and ambiguity) is 'Reinvention'. This is what has been discussed in this section. In simple terms, 'Reinvention' is an action/or process of changing something so that it transforms into something new and better.

One of the primary causes for the downfall of companies is their complacent attitude and arrogance, basking on their laurels to even thinks of failures and an unwillingness to learn. That is why a continuous learning and reinvention approach can prevent disasters. The message for organizations and economies is to 'Be in motion to set the pace for the race for a smooth momentum'.

So, how do we know that we need to reinvent ourselves? The S curve, which depicts successive stages of start-up, growth, scale-up, and maturity, is the ideal representation of any business life cycle. There are also inflexion points on the S curve that, like icebergs in a ship's path, cannot be avoided but can be navigated with proper planning and preparation. Top performers successfully transition from maturity to growth stages by anticipating inflexion points, whereas others who are unaware risk sinking.

Organizations must monitor checkpoints to determine where they stand. There are some diagnostic tools for this, which are listed below:

a. **Plan ahead of time** - are the signal sources for market disruptions and feedback the same, or have they changed, and are employees less engaged in sharing market insights? Do businesses have false beliefs about their talent pool and market dominance, a lack of knowledge and awareness of new entrants and technology, and are reactive rather than proactive?

b. **Developing a change strategy** - are anti-change and sceptical of new products, solutions, or methods.

c. **Implement change** - rarely handled or exposed to change execution, a limited commitment of resources and lack of system, ineffective executives, high inertia, and low motivation within the organization.

   If the majority of the responses on this diagnostic tool are yes, it is a clear indication that reinvention is required. The timing of when to reinvent is also critical, as discussed further in this section.

   Then there is the 'Strategic lever' framework to know when and how to reinvent. These include competition, industry position, organization performance indicators

(KPIs), customer needs, business models, talents, and capabilities.

Reinvention is thus a continuous process in an organization, with the leadership and management teams playing a critical role in initiating reinvention and change management.

Now let us see what is required from the organization set-up point of view -

- A system that aligns the organization's growth plans across functions to survive today and thrive for tomorrow's successes. Furthermore, the top management team must maintain a high pitch for organizational reinvention and embed this culture throughout all functions. Plus, focused resources and an organizational structure to match.

PART III

Innovation and Disciplined
Execution for Assured Success

It was a get-together dinner that Bharti was hosting for friends. There would be 20 people altogether, including men, women, and children. Though it was impossible to prepare all the dishes at home, she decided to make some snacks and serve them hot when the guests arrived. She had completed all the shopping one day prior so that she would be relaxed on the day of the party. Finally, the day arrived, and as planned, she started preparing the starter snack (cauliflower Manchurian). She was halfway through the process when to her utter despair, she realized that one of the important ingredients (corn flour) for the dish was missing. She was sure she had purchased it, but it was nowhere to be found!!

Don't we all face similar situations in our everyday lives? Anyone would have felt the jitters in any other space or time as the party was about to begin in half an hour. However, the fact that Swiggy delivery services deliver groceries within 10 to 15 minutes brought a smile and a sigh of relief.

An outcome of innovation, Swiggy's facility is relatively new, but it has grown in popularity due to the fact that they deliver products quickly and come to the aid of customers in distress. The company, which is already commercialized, began as a food delivery app and diversified into this instant service in response to changing market demands in order to meet customers' needs. What would normally take 6 to 24 hours is now reduced to a few minutes at the click of a button.

And how was all of this made possible? By improvising and changing their business model and strategy. The company established numerous warehouses throughout the city to ensure that every location was covered. Despite the challenges, they were able to meet customer expectations and solve their problem. Even though this has not been very profitable, that is what innovation is about.

Chapter I

Starting the Journey of Innovation – Means to Create the BLUE Ocean

"I believe you have to be willing to be misunderstood
if you're treading the path of innovation."

~Jeff Bezos, Founder of Amazon

There are two primary aspects to innovation: an "innovative idea" and a "valuable" innovative idea. Let's look at these two aspects.

"The value of an idea lies in the use of it."

~Thomas Edison

Source: clipart-library.com

A new study conducted by psychologists at Queen's University in Canada suggests that an average human has around 6200 thoughts in a single day. If we take out the time and write down all the thoughts that pass through our minds, we could write a book each day! Imagine the endless creative potential when these 6200 thoughts intertwine with one another. Multiple studies show that certain individuals are more likely to generate novel, useful, and creative ideas regardless of their field of expertise or job title.

However, creativity is not enough on its own. The next step is to develop, produce, and implement the idea. This is why there are many latent innovators who may have highly creative ideas but are unable to turn them into action.

There is a thin line between an innovative idea and a valuable innovative idea, and that thin subtle difference is "**Execution**". Execution is the capacity to turn an innovative idea into a successful service, product, or venture. William

James, an American Philosopher, Historian, and Psychologist, said, "truth is something that happens to an idea". Regardless of how creative, opportunistic, or proactive you are. Thus the ability to propel innovation requires a different mindset.

Take a look around. You will see many people at your workplace or in your family who come out with new ideas every day. They invest countless hours planning and refining their ideas but never get a chance to start the innovation process. Basically, fail to put it into action.

Regardless of the magnitude of your idea, it is utterly worthless unless brought to fruition. The previous chapter delved into the generation of ingenious ideas and their manifestation in the form of innovation. This chapter will showcase strategies to transform your innovative idea into a profitable reality.

Now, sometimes when you innovate, you tend to make mistakes. Does that mean failure?

Not really! It is best to figure out the loopholes and move forward quickly.

Innovation needs constant improvisation that keeps fitting into the changing cultures. So unless your product or service doesn't solve a pressing problem or make incremental improvements to the quality of life, it is just a figment of a dream. If you have a thousand ideas and one turns out to be good, then you need to use this one idea to change people's lives. Let's look at various aspects that will help you as an innovator to commercialize your precious ideas.

An Entrepreneurial mindset

An entrepreneurial mindset comprises a set of principles, thought processes, and perspectives that fuel entrepreneurial actions. Entrepreneurship entails the transformation of imaginative ideas into practical innovations.

"Wantrepreneurs" spend their time reading, watching videos, and crafting plans, but they fail to take decisive action and execute. Entrepreneurs, however, are driven by action. As the entrepreneurial icon Walt Disney once said, "The way to get started is to quit talking and begin doing."

Fun Play

Cultivating an entrepreneurial mindset requires daily dedication to personal development. By examining your behaviour and learning how to align your thought patterns with your objectives, you can cultivate this vital mindset. We have compiled a list of powerful words that embody the core essence of the entrepreneurial mindset.

As the adage goes, we are what we repeatedly do. Thus, reading these words may inspire you to start your day on a productive note. However, before diving in, take a moment to assess your own strength in each of these areas. For instance, you may see yourself as highly self-motivated and goal-oriented but perhaps struggle with self-acceptance.

Ask yourself, what can I do to increase self-awareness?

How will 'Self Awareness' help me in the long run?

How does it make me a better entrepreneur?

As you ponder on these questions, you will realize the importance of each and every attribute. When it comes to pursuing a successful innovation, the right mindset is just as important as marketing or distribution. So let's have a look at traits that help develop an entrepreneurial mindset.

An opportunistic mindset

Opportunities are at the heart of entrepreneurship and innovation, and some people are much more alert to them than others. For example, Frank McNamara got the idea to co-found **Diners Club** credit cards in 1950 when he once had to pay a restaurant bill but realized he did not have cash in his pocket.

In the late 1960s, John Adrian Shepherd-Barron hit upon the idea of creating **ATMs** to solve the problem he faced of being unable to go to the bank during office hours to withdraw cash. His model of cash dispensers was inspired by chocolate-bar vending machines.

A healthy dose of risk

Contrary to popular belief, successful innovators are often more methodical and cautious but possess an above-average appetite for risk compared to the general population. Consider the following case of risky innovation.

Being attuned to your surroundings and harnessing your creativity can also lead to the discovery of novel uses for products or the identification of unintended consequences. This is exactly what happened with Pfizer, a pharmaceutical company, when they stumbled upon the potential of "sildenafil citrate," which eventually became the blockbuster drug **Viagra.**

Similarly, rod wax was once an "unvalued petroleum by product" in the oil industry before British chemist Robert Chesebrough discovered its ability to heal cuts and burns suffered by oil workers. After years of refining experiments, he went on to create **Vaseline.** These examples demonstrate that in addition to identifying a problem, timely execution is crucial for success.

Proactivity and Perseverance

These traits allow innovators to capitalize on opportunities they identify. Successful innovators are more driven, resilient, and energetic than their peers. Perseverance means consistently striving towards a goal or task until it is achieved, an attitude of never surrendering! It was this tenacity that led Thomas Edison to famously say, "I didn't fail 1000 times," after numerous attempts to invent the light bulb.

Formal education or training

These are crucial for recognizing new opportunities. However, contrary to popular belief, even though some successful innovators may be dropout geniuses, many are highly trained experts in their field. Society often assumes that without expertise, it is difficult to differentiate between relevant and irrelevant information or to distinguish between noise and signals.

The lack of formal education allowed Thomas Edison to challenge conventional wisdom. When a partially deaf four-year-old boy returned home with a note from his teacher saying, "Your Tommy is too stupid to learn. Get him out of school," his mother replied, "My Tommy is not too stupid to learn. I will teach him myself." That boy grew up to become the renowned inventor Thomas Edison, who had only three months of formal education. However, in those days, traditional education was often too rigid, leading to what is known as 'tunnel vision.' In Edison's case, the lack of formal education allowed him to think freely and outside the box.

This scenario was prevalent back in the early days. However, today society has evolved to be more pragmatic and solution-focused, inviting more novel ideas and new ways of functioning. Did you know that Microsoft was started in a garage by two intelligent, creative people who turned it into a multinational billion-dollar company? To pay homage to its origin, the company turned Bill Gates's old office into something called 'The Garage'. The place filled with every tech toy and world-class tool imaginable is open to all Microsoft employees. The employees are encouraged to use the space to work on their pet projects, and special 'Garage weeks' are organized for each product team.

"Innovation takes birth in sync with the evolution of customers' expectations and demands or vice versa. Either way, organizations around the world have to continually innovate themselves and keep up with people's wants."

~Ketan Kapoor, Co-founder of Mercer-Metti

Innovation success rates

Research shows that a staggering 60-80% of new products meet with failure. Oftentimes, we are unable to discern the best course of action in innovation. Consider the case of **Opioid Painkillers.** Pharmaceutical companies began producing these drugs with the intention of relieving chronic pain in patients. However, the mass production and widespread over-prescription of these medications led to dependency, addiction, and, ultimately, the "opioid crisis" in the United States. This innovation has been deemed one of the most detrimental in history, causing thousands of deaths and tearing apart families.

At this point, you must be wondering why we are focusing on failure.

There are numerous stories of innovation out there, so why focus on companies that got it wrong? Well, every innovator starts with an idea that seems perfect and doable but eventually, it fails. It could be related to the quality of an idea itself, its implementation, or internal organizational causes.

The business environment today is very dynamic and competitive, and new product development is a crucial process. You may start with a simple product idea on a napkin. Next, you start making calls and, maybe in a few months, begin the process. But the journey from napkins to the product being launched in the market is unique. Let me take you through each important step of this journey.

What is Innovation?

By definition, *"Innovation"* is a useful application of Invention or combining ideas in a new and useful way, offering a significant change to users. Innovation is many times a new or improved product, solution, service, or combination of all enhancing user experience. The cycle of innovation starts with *creativity and applying imagination to solve a problem or challenge.*

The word innovation is also explained by the Latin root *nova,* which means "New".

A famous economist described the economic, societal, and organizational impact of innovation as "winds of creative destruction", sweeping away both old ways of doing things and the enterprises and institutions clinging to those old thoughts.

"Creativity is seeing the same thing but thinking differently."

– Dr. APJ Abdul Kalam

The cycle of Ideation to Commercialisation

IDEATION simply means generating ideas. This process is always encouraged, shared, and built upon. Ideas are praised with the following consideration in mind.

- What's good about the idea?

- What are the good things that might result?

- How does it add customer value or reduce cost?

With enough consensus that an idea has potential, a project is defined, and the next step begins!

Let's look at four broad areas again.

- ***Definition phase*** – It is where you do the technical analysis and spot the opportunity or gap in the market or unmet needs of customers.

- ***Ideation phase*** – It is where you identify and analyze various solution concepts to meet customer, business, and technical requirements.

- ***Demonstration Phase*** – In this phase, you demonstrate the feasibility of the selected concept(s) for meeting the customer, business, and technical requirements.

- ***Transfer to Commercialization*** – In this phase, the selected concept is incorporated into an actual product application, a strategy to commercialize.

So technically, the process starts with some 'informal' ideation (Definition phase), followed by an extensive 'ideation' phase, where the idea is further developed after identifying needs, requirements, project plan, team members, etc.

You see, ideation is not just the introduction of a concept. It includes everything necessary to start investing in and creating prototypes for demonstration purposes.

Now the journey from ideation to commercialization is both an exciting and challenging endeavour. When we are developing a new product, we need to identify certain steps that will help us get started from the initial concept to the final market launch. The process explained here is generic, unlike the very specific approach of "Design Thinking" explained in other parts of this book.

Step 1: Idea Generation (Ideation)

This is the first stage of the product development process that begins by generating new product ideas. As mentioned in detail above, the initial idea stage is where you brainstorm product concepts based on customer needs, pricing, and market research. Here are some elements to keep in mind while going through Stage 1.

1. **Target market:** Your target market is the consumer profile you're building your product for.

2. **Existing products:** When you have a new product concept, it's a good idea to evaluate your existing product portfolio.

    Are there existing products that solve a similar problem?

    If so, is your new concept different enough to be viable?

3. **Functionality:** It is important to identify what functions the new product will serve. Consider the look and feel of your product and why someone would be interested in purchasing it.

4. **SWOT Analysis:** Analyzing your product strengths, weaknesses, opportunities, and threats early in the process can help you build the best version of your new concept. Conducting a SWOT Analysis ensures your product is different from competitors and solves a market gap.

5. **SCAMPER Method:** In order to refine your idea, use brainstorming methods like SCAMPER, which involves Substituting, Combining, Adapting, Modifying,

Putting to another use, Eliminating, or Rearranging your product concept.

"Unlearn to learn" should be the motto when we are innovating! To get fresh, new ideas, we must have another look at our pre-built assumptions and challenge our mental model.

Step 2: Product Definition

Once you have understood your target market and product functionality, it's time to define the product. This is also referred to as **scoping or concept development**. During this stage, it's important to look into the following details.

- **Business analysis:** A business analysis consists of mapping out a distribution strategy, e-commerce strategy, and more in-depth competitor analysis in the chosen market.

- **Value proposition:** A value proposition outlines the specific problem that a product is solving and how it does so differently. This value can be leveraged for market research and in crafting a marketing strategy and market positioning.

- **Success metrics:** It is essential to clarify success metrics early so you can evaluate and measure success once the product is launched.

- **Marketing strategy:** Once you've identified your value proposition and success metrics, begin brainstorming a marketing strategy that fits your needs. Consider which channels you want to promote your product on—such as social media or a blog post.

Once these ideas have been defined, it's time to begin the initial prototyping.

Step 3: Prototyping

During the prototyping phase, your team will conduct in-depth research and documentation of the product, developing a more comprehensive concept and constructing a physical or digital prototype. These early prototypes may range from simple sketches to complex computer renderings of the initial design.

Here are the following things you keep in mind.

- **Market risk research:** It is important to analyze any potential risks associated with the production of your product before it is physically created.

- **Development strategy:** Next, you can begin working through your development plan, assigning tasks and timelines.

- **Feasibility analysis:** The next step in the process is to evaluate your product strategy based on feasibility. Determine if the scoping and estimated timeline are possible to accomplish.

- **MVP:** The ultimate result of the prototyping stage is the creation of a minimum viable product (MVP). For instance, an MVP bike might include a frame, wheels, and a seat but not yet feature a basket or bell. Developing an MVP allows your team to launch the product more quickly than building all desired features at once, which can delay launch timelines.

The strategy should be to create the MVP first and then gather feedback from customers and other stakeholders. Customer feedback is paramount. Once you have an understanding of what customers do and do not prefer, make adjustments accordingly and finalize the product. Adhering to these steps can be incredibly helpful in conserving resources.

Step 4: Initial Design

During the initial design phase, you collaborate with project stakeholders to create a mock-up of the product based on the MVP. A successful product design may require several rounds of iteration, so it is important to

- **Source materials:** This may involve working with various vendors to order materials or creating them in-house.

- **Communicate with stakeholders:** This includes providing regular progress reports to share updates and seek approvals as needed while gathering initial feedback. Once the design is complete, ask senior management and project stakeholders for their initial thoughts.

- **Revise the product design:** Do this as and when necessary until the final version is ready to be developed and implemented.

Once the design is approved and ready to be executed, move on to the validation phase for final testing before launching the product.

Step 5: Validation and Testing

This step guarantees that every aspect of the product, from development to marketing, is functioning optimally before it is released to the public. To ensure the quality of your product, follow these steps:

- **Concept development and testing:** You may have successfully designed your prototype, but you'll still need to work through any issues that arise while developing the concept.

- **Front-end testing:** During this stage, test the front-end functionality for risks with development code or consumer-facing errors.

- **Test marketing:** Before you begin producing your final product, test your marketing plan for functionality and errors.

Step 6: Commercialisation

It is now time to commercialize your concept, which involves launching your product. Commercialization is the process of introducing new products or services to the market and encompasses production, distribution, marketing, sales, customer support, and other essential functions vital to achieving the commercial success of the new product or service.

During this stage, you will focus on-

- **Product development:** This is the physical creation of your product that will be released to customers. This may involve the production or further development of software concepts.

- **Supply chain, Go-to-Market, and E-commerce implementation:** Once the product has been developed and you are ready to launch, your development team will transition your e-commerce materials to a live state.

Here are some real-life examples of the above processes—How successful companies went from ideation to commercialization.

How Uber solved a market gap.

While Uber is now widely considered the leading ride-sharing service, this was not always the case. They began with a strong product strategy that helped them become the innovative company they are today. Uber's strategy started by addressing a gap in the existing taxi industry (**STEP 1**) by streamlining the ride-hailing process and simplifying payment processing. However, they did not stop there. They continue to innovate their product portfolio by offering a range of ride tiers, from luxury to budget-friendly, or by introducing Uber Meals (**STEP 2**).

A useful technique for enhancing creativity is to approach inspiration as a process, with these three simple components:

- Break down the idea into a series of tasks

- Measure and track the tasks

- Analyze the outcome

Innovation Types

Typically, there are two types of innovation for products, solutions, or services: Incremental Innovation and Radical Innovation, which differ in their level of impact.

1. **Incremental innovations:** These are meant to provide enhancements to existing or current products or solutions, improving user experiences or efficiency. They are often implemented using existing technologies or structures. An example of incremental innovation is improving the fuel efficiency of a car through minor modifications to the transmission system. Another example is increasing the speed of a computer's central processor without fundamentally changing PC technologies. Incremental innovations are characterized by improvements to current technologies, business growth in current markets, enhanced customer experience, and the introduction of new elements.

2. **Radical innovations:** Radical innovations offer something entirely new to the world through technology, structure, or methods. They are also known as disruptive technology innovations when driven by new technology. Other terms for radical innovations include breakthrough innovation or discontinuous innovations.

An example of radical innovation is the internet, which revolutionized global communication. Electric vehicles (EVs) as an alternative to fossil fuel-powered vehicles are other examples of disruptive technology innovation. A transformation in display technology from cathode ray tube to LCD (liquid crystal displays) is another example, as well as the latest versions of touch screen displays on smartphones and laptops.

Disruptive technologies disrupt relevant existing technologies and the enterprises that rely on them, often establishing new business models that displace older technologies. When radical innovations are transformed into commercially viable products, they create new markets. Although businesses that emerge from disruptive innovation may start small, they have a high potential for growth as early adopters and lead users begin to adopt and promote them.

Disruptive innovations may also emerge from very minor or small changes in technology, but based on business models. For example, Netflix, Uber, Adobe subscription models, and Amazon all offered new business models that leveraged the internet. These disruptive innovations disrupted many existing enterprises.

One research institute, Rensselaer Polytechnic, defined the criteria for classification as a radical innovation when one or more of the following characteristics are met:

- An entirely new set of performance parameters

- Improvements in known performance parameters by 5x or more (e.g. computational speed, data transmission rates)

- A significant reduction in cost, more than 30% from current levels.

There are good possibilities that radical innovation could potentially change the basis of competition, too, in addition to the above.

Usually, innovations within an industry or organization are characterized by a series of incremental innovations punctuated by occasional radical innovations over time. A balanced mix of incremental innovations improves efficiency and supports short-term financial results, while radical innovations prepare for the future and create niche support organizations, leading to market leadership. Therefore, a synergy between the current core and a balanced innovation portfolio for the future is necessary.

Incremental innovations pose little risk, have a shorter timeline for return on investment, and may provide a consistent stream of income in existing markets and technologies. They help maintain profitability, meet customer needs, retain market share, and are less expensive. However, it is important to focus on customer benefits rather than just adding multiple features to avoid the risk of competitors taking away market share.

Radical innovations require a long period of investment with patience, resources, and the potential risk of failure. Successful radical innovations bring organizations to the forefront of the market, industry-sweeping reforms, and high returns on investment.

Product and Process innovations: Innovation can come from both the creation of new products and improvements to processes. Often, innovations are focused on new products. But sometimes, they come from changes in the way something is made. Without the right process or manufacturing ability, a promising new product idea may be doomed to fail. That's why it's crucial to consider both the product and the process when seeking innovation. Process innovations in manufacturing and assembly have helped make products like cars, steel, and diapers successful.

Service Innovations: Revolutionary service innovations that significantly improve customer experiences can completely change the business model of an industry. For example, Southwest Airlines, with its low-cost services targeting travelers who would normally use cars or buses, was able to disrupt the airline industry. They accomplished this by offering low fares, frequent flights, fast turnaround times, and a compelling value proposition to customers.

Another example is of UBER taxi service, which helps you to hire taxis at your convenience while enhancing the user experience for taxi booking, payments, and tracking. This service innovation altered the taxi service industry in a big way, making many of them obsolete to the extent that a fleet of taxis was shifted and attached to UBER services.

Another example is the digital payment app PAYTM, which has made cashless transactions easy and widely accepted in India for everything from small shops to big malls and taxi rides.

As we have discussed various categories of innovation, it is important to discuss the crucial type known as reverse innovation.

Reverse Innovation: Generally, innovation efforts and outcomes typically originate and are implemented in developed nations, particularly in the West.

The concept of Reverse Innovation, first coined by professors Vijay Govindarajan and Chris Trimble from Dartmouth Tuck University in 2009, addresses this notion.

In normal cases, whenever a product is innovated for developed nations, adapting it for developing or poorer economies may be challenging. This can be due to affordability or operating environments like the atmosphere, power supply qualities, and other infrastructural readiness.

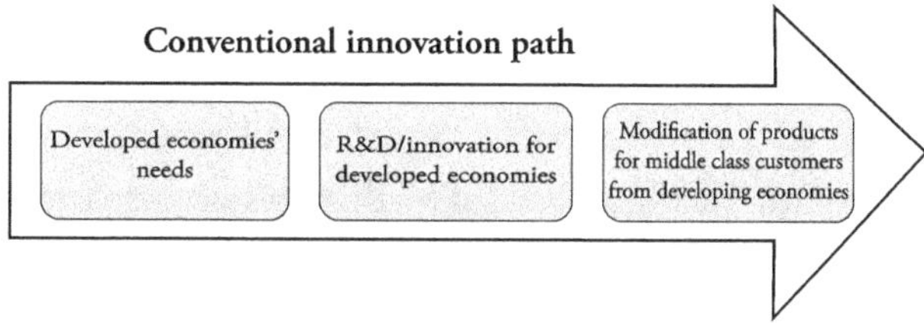

Multinational entrepreneurs often resort to cutting functions or altering forms in order to make their products more affordable for consumers in developing countries. However, this approach may not always be effective in addressing affordability issues or reaching large target markets in these nations.

Glocalization, or the production and distribution of products in local markets with or without adjustments for local customer needs, maybe a more viable option for the top end of the market in developing countries with similar needs and resources as those in developed markets.

Customers in emerging markets often seek fully-featured products at prices that are proportionate to their income levels. In countries with a growing middle and upper middle class,

such as India, there is a significant demand for products and solutions that are common in developed markets but at more affordable prices. For example, it may be necessary to offer these products at 50% of the price charged in developed nations while only incurring 25% of the cost.

So, having a large market potential in developing markets, in order to be successful there, product innovation needs to happen there by having a close understanding of the market and developing the local ecosystem.

Living in an interconnected global economy, these innovations and outcomes can be extended to other markets, including matured markets. This will also need calibration of a matured market mindset about innovations out of emerging markets and a willingness to reframe the assumptions.

A right approach of having both glocalization and a set of Reverse Innovation projects would offer great growth opportunities and profitably address new areas of growth.

Some of the most impactful examples of Reverse innovations include-

- GE's creation of the portable, low-cost GE MAC 400 ECG machine for rural populations in need of affordable healthcare. This innovative solution was later improved and released in the U.S. as the MAC 800. By targeting the Indian market and overcoming challenges such as transporting bulky ECG machines, availability of electricity, and cost barriers, GE was able to produce portable ECGs for a large population in need.

- TATA Motors in India introduced the TATA Nano, a cost-effective car with huge potential for Reverse innovation in developed markets.

Likewise, many multinational companies have established R&D and product development centres in India to target the local market and later expand globally.

- Bosch in India has one of its largest R&D setups outside Germany, serving customers on a global scale. As an example, the company's telematic solution called iTraMS (intelligent transportation management system) was developed in India and has been implemented with an Indian original equipment manufacturer. The software allows fleet-owners to effectively manage their fleet of vehicles

- Coca-Cola's Minute Maid's Pulpy, a popular orange juice with pulp in China, was introduced in other countries as well.

- Tata's Swach, a cheap and effective water purifier, was launched in the Indian rural market. Swach means clean in the Indian national language Hindi. This product uses paddy husk ash as a filter and silver nanotechnology to purify water without the need for running water, electricity, or boiling. It can provide a family of five with purified drinking water for a year and has the potential to create a whole new market.

Summary

As stated earlier in this book, simply having an idea will not result in anything unless that idea is carried out. We know that humans have a lot of thoughts, which leads to great ideas. But, an idea is useless unless it improves people's lives and is commercialized.

One of the most important ways to achieve success in this field is to cultivate an entrepreneurial mindset. And the good news is that this can be learned! An entrepreneurial mindset is a set of beliefs, thought processes, and worldview that drives entrepreneurial behaviour. According to studies repeating certain powerful words every day, like, 'not afraid of failures, 'learning-oriented,' 'driven and tenacious,' and so on, helps in developing an entrepreneurial mindset.

Apart from that opportunistic mindset, self-awareness, risk-taking abilities, proactive persistence, and formal training are essential requisites.

The entire process of innovation, from ideation to commercialization, is covered in this chapter. Ideation or idea generation is followed by Concept Development, prototyping, initial design, validation and testing, and finally, commercialization.

Also featured here are different types of Innovations:

- Incremental Innovation aims to improve existing products or services.

- Radical innovation - introduces completely new things to the world, such as technology or methods.

- Product and process innovation

- Services Innovation entails increasing the efficiency of customer services.

- Reverse Innovation - an innovation that takes into consideration the economic criteria, affordability, especially for developing nations, and the product developed for developing markets having the potential to be adapted to matured markets.

Chapter II

Leveraging Strategy as the Key Driver – A Multidimensional Approach for Continued Momentum

In the previous chapter, we focused on understanding the basics of innovation, the kinds of innovation, and also the pros and cons of different kinds. While the need for innovation programs feels extremely important, the chances of making a successful innovation are rare or low.

Although many organizations have structured processes for strategizing, innovation tends to take a back seat due to the pressing need to focus on immediate concerns and meet short-term goals. However, with the right approach, a carefully crafted strategy can serve as a catalyst for fostering innovation within an organization. In this chapter, we will understand how a well-crafted strategy itself can be leveraged to drive great innovation journeys across organizations.

"In the modern world of business, it is useless to be a creative, original thinker unless you can also sell what you create. Management cannot be expected to recognize a good idea unless it is presented to them by a good salesman."

~David Ogilvy

When we use the term 'Innovation Strategy', we mean the steps companies take to bring life to their vision and improve business growth. They can also be seen as a set of coherent, mutually reinforcing policies or behaviours aimed at achieving a specific competitive goal.

Consider this.

Your company has various departments – The sales department is concerned about the pressing needs of the biggest customers. The marketing department will see opportunities to leverage the brand through complementary products or to expand market share through new distribution channels. Business unit heads are focused on their target markets and their funding pressures. R&D scientists and engineers tend to see opportunities in new technologies.

When leaders are too busy trying to create better results for the day, it's easy for innovation to fall by the wayside because of the absence of a clear strategic framework. Without a clear, long-term plan in place, it's hard for an organization to thrive in the future. This can lead to a cycle of panic, with leaders making hasty, reactive decisions in an effort to keep the company's innovation afloat.

In order to be a successful enterprise on a long-term basis, it is necessary to have a so-called *"ambidexterity"* set-up in the organization that focuses on both the present and future at the same time. This reinvention approach towards innovation enables sustained S-curves of growth and retains market leadership positions.

Facing unprecedented competition and rapid technological change in a borderless, interconnected global economy, organizations may turn to tried-and-true strategies to stay in the game. The ease of access to information can also play a role in this process. The reality is this survival strategy on past successes may no longer work in our favour. When *"exploring"* new becomes highly essential, current challenges demand an over-the-top level of attention to efficiently manage both *"exploitation"* and *"explorations"* to create the *"wished to be"* futures.

An organization's strategy should allow it to focus on both exploration (innovation) and exploitation (control) at the same time. However, it can be difficult to balance these two priorities and integrate them into a unified approach.

Instead of swinging back and forth between the two, it's important to find a way to integrate them into a single, cohesive strategy.

Ray Stata, cofounder of Analog Devices, a more than 2 Billion Dollar Company that had lived through such challenges, shares, *"I came to the conclusion long ago that limits to innovation have less to do with technology or creativity than organizational agility. Inspired individuals can only do so much." Emphasis must shift: from ideas to execution and from leadership excellence to organizational excellence.*

New Company Creating Successful Strategies

Let's take the example of Airbnb, one of the fastest-growing tech companies. It has quite possibly changed the way we travel forever. It all began with co-founders Brian and Joe renting out 3 air mattresses on their apartment's floor. They made $80 per guest. It seemed like a great idea for a startup, so they launched a website and invited other people to list their own mattresses for hire.

They got a few bookings here and there, but things didn't go well. Sometime later, they identified the most likely problem. The co-founders grabbed their cameras and visited every one of their NYC listings. They persuaded the owners to let them take a ton of photographs of their places. The photographs were edited slightly and uploaded to the website. Within a month of starting this strategy, sales doubled and then tripled. The rest is history.

Airbnb's story shows that business strategies don't have to be grand and super long-term affairs. Living, striving today, and preparing for tomorrow are some important steps of innovation. Therefore, your company's strategy currently may revolve around a specific challenge preventing the business from taking off. Once the challenge is solved, the company progresses on its roadmap.

The next question is - Do all companies have to be new to run a successful innovation? How about a company, already a successful one, would it pursue innovation for a new business or segment?

How Important Is Developing A Good Innovation Strategy For An Organisation?

"The best way to predict the future is to invent it."

~Steve Jobs

In this new "digital age", we are witnessing a gradual but inexorable shift in both developed and developing economies. Manufacturing, Trading, Information Sector, Communication, and Service Sectors all have experienced rising consumer expectations.

In today's market, where product life cycles are shorter, and access to the global market is easier, small, agile companies can quickly predict and meet changing demands. To drive innovation and succeed in new businesses, organizations need more than just ideas and creativity. They also need to do the following with the drive and determination to perform well.

- Identify weak signals that emerge before something disruptive lands. (E.g., the Internet didn't explode overnight, but over the years; some businessmen could sense ahead)

- Clearly identify non-linear shifts happening around wherein customers become competitors or non-traditional competitors. Notice the shifts in distribution channels (online, offline channels), demographical shifts, new laws or sanctions getting introduced, the emergence of new technology, or fading out of some of the current technologies.

- Clearly articulate strategic intent, motivation, and challenges.

- Identify strategic levers that bring significant customer value, defendable for the short-midterm horizon.

- Bring a balanced focus on managing current business and future horizon connected with innovation (Ideation to commercialization cycle).

- Make sure the crafted strategies are executed strongly into successful innovations.

Having An Excellent Product Or Service Is Mandatory But Is That The Only Prerequisite For A Successful Innovation?

A small or mid-sized organization often innovates good products, but that alone does not guarantee success. What is further needed is a pro-innovation culture - tools, strategies, and processes that work on creating new value for which customers are willing to pay.

Le's see how an effective innovation strategy is designed to fulfill the necessary goals.

- **Clarify priorities and goals.**

  An innovation strategy outlines the goals of the organization's innovation activities and helps focus efforts on reaching those goals.

  For example, Apple builds innovations by acquiring startups and partnering with other companies to develop new products, such as a partnership with Volkswagen to produce driverless shuttle vans for employees. The company also has an internal accelerator

that leverages Apple employees to push forward new research projects, such as Titan, an electric car project.

- **Foster alignment.**

  With a plan in place, diverse groups within an organization will all be working toward common goals rather than pursuing their individual priorities.

  Amazon, in addition to an innovation lab that creates new hardware devices such as the Kindle and Echo, also encourages all employees to pitch innovative ideas. For example, an employee spontaneously pitched the idea for Amazon Prime in a memo, and leaders provided internal funding to make it happen.

- **Keep a business from resting on its laurels.**

  Even businesses that start as innovators must continue to innovate strategically, otherwise, copycats and innovative competitors are likely to take market share over time.

  The best example is Google. The company offers innovation classes for employees and runs an R&D facility that has launched products like self-driving cars and Google Glass. But the company also looks to bring in innovations from external sources, with GV, its own venture capital fund for innovative start-ups, and an incubator for promising entrepreneurs.

- **Help a business achieve long-term success.**

  Without ongoing innovation, a company is unlikely to gain (or maintain) a competitive advantage or keep customers engaged over the long term.

Therefore, aligning innovation with business strategy is important as it gives you a better understanding of your competitors. Your innovation strategy should answer the questions of what unique value you will bring to your market. In short, what types of innovations will allow you to capture the market and bring value propositions?

Strategy is itself an enabler for innovation to come out strongly. **Your strategy provides the necessary laser focus answer on "why" you innovate, "what" to focus on, and "how" to successfully organize this.**

The best strategic plans are always flexible. As customer needs and market needs change, we adapt innovation strategies to better fit reality. Long story short, strategic planning and innovation go hand in hand.

Now let us discuss another important element which is very relevant in the global business world of the 21st century.

Managing The Current And Creating The Future

Any organization today is required to fulfil two contradictory objectives - *exploitation* and *exploration*. Maintaining dual attention on these two activities is crucial in order to survive and excel in the present, secure the future, and create sustainable growth. But managing this duality is a challenge.

For example, start-ups that are too focused on exploring the new, and engaged in too much experimentation in the process, lose the scope of exploiting the outputs of their exploration activities.

To clarify, Exploration refers to the discovery of new products, resources, knowledge, and opportunities, and it is associated with radical changes and learning through experimentation. Whereas, Exploitation refers to the refinement of existing products, resources, knowledge, and competencies and is associated with incremental changes and learning through local search (Benner & Tushman, 2003; March 1991).

> *"To sustain excellence, companies need dual strategies—one for the present and one for the future."*
>
> **~Abell, 1999**

It is very important to build dualities in an organization. Or what is also known as 'ambidexterity capability', an organization's ability to perform exploration and exploit tasks at the same time, as referred to at the beginning of this chapter.

Unlike organizations that are solely focused on innovation, here, the leaders and managers have to continuously shift their priorities from one to another. Here is an example of how a big company works as a dual organization.

Apple

For years, Apple has been known to be excellent at exploiting new technologies, adapting them, and using consumer insights to support the user base, constantly updating their products with new features and bringing continuous improvements. In short, they are the prime master of exploitation.

However, Apple also does an excellent job of exploiting its position in its app store through its supply chain, customer service, and its personalized services in the Apple Retail Stores. It has now become the master of engagement, extracting and exploiting all touch points in its customer base while also exploring numerous new boundaries for this customer engagement process.

They are exemplary exploiters and equally real explorers, as they are seeking ways to use technology, design, and functionality in completely different, market-shaping ways. Their objective is to extend and attract new users but lock in loyalty as well.

Today, businesses are constantly evolving. Most companies try to live the dual agenda, or otherwise, they fail. As a leader, you must take an ambidextrous approach. Balancing exploitation with exploring is managing often opposing tensions that help resolve tension at the heart of the business. However, it is easier said than done.

It is not easy to switch one *off* and the other one *on* in complex organizational settings or well-established structures. We need to separate the actions of exploit and explore *consciously*. It is not like our often unconscious ability to simply switch hands or the way we make a conscious change in our thinking when we prepare to adapt and adjust mentally for these different activities at a personal level.

Now let's look at an aspect where most organizations pay attention but do not leverage it fully.

The Three-Pronged Approach

Prof. Vijay Govindarajan, also known as VG, a strategy expert in one of his books, "A Strategy for Leading Innovation", introduced the concept of THREE-BOX solutions, which is

a three-pronged approach. The information in this section is based on that book, and credit for the original ideas goes to VG.

Often organizations spend most of their time placing dominant emphasis on managing the present but fail to invest wisely in the future. While the future is unpredictable, we can plan the predictable. Three-box solutions concept is characterized by setting aside certain beliefs of the past, assumptions, and practices that would otherwise become a barrier to scaling new heights of tomorrow and its future potential.

The image shows wherein each of these corners of the triangle (of a future enterprise) keeps itself in shape. Any missing elements of forgetting the past and creating the future make the triangle a skewed one and a real challenge for the existence of the organization, e.g., heavily loading on Box-1 emphasizing current business may neglect other boxes.

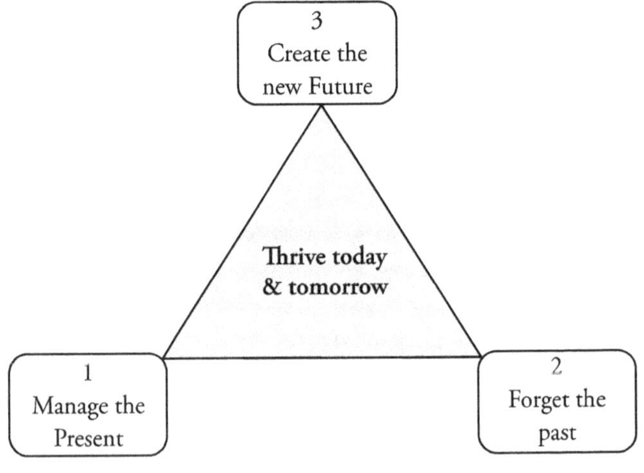

Box 1 is the "performance engine" that supports the company's daily operations and generates profits. This box helps the company manage its core business efficiently and profitably. It also allows for small, incremental changes to meet market demands and focuses on short-term goals. Leadership here focuses on setting challenging goals to improve efficiency and performance, reduce costs and address any problems quickly. The culture is one of smart, cheap, and fast decision-making.

Box 2 is meant to "forget the past" and focus on practices that support the current business but do not support new business or innovation. This box helps the company avoid being trapped by its current successes and allows it to adapt to a changing business environment. It creates space and structure for the future and helps the company start building for tomorrow. Leadership in this box focuses on finding opportunities, setting good examples for experimentation, and creating an environment that supports innovation.

Box 3 is for innovation and generating breakthrough ideas that create the future with new products and businesses. The new future is built with certain assumptions, risks, a set of hypotheses with available information on the market, target on-boarding non-customers, the extent of risks on outcomes, choosing or scoping out the right idea and solution, etc. The leadership focuses here on more qualitative, long-term impacts on the journey, learning of failures, commitments to execute tasks, testing assumptions, redeploying resources, market development, etc. Progress is not focused just on revenue during early time horizons to keep the business evolving.

Skill sets and resources needed for Box-1 and Box-3 would be different, hence choosing the right resources is the key recipe for success.

With the right balancing and the emphasis on these boxes, a business can pivot successfully over time, outpacing market dynamics.

Forgetting, Borrowing, and Learning

> *"The arrogance of success is to think that what you did yesterday will be sufficient for tomorrow."*
>
> ~William Pollard

The biggest challenge organizations face is balancing these three areas, especially when success on current business is peaking, delivering extremely good results month over month, quarter to quarter. This will lead to more and more difficulties in executing breakthrough strategies for the future, a sign that reflects the success trap.

Leadership and the rest of the organization start applying the same set of rules on hiring, compensation, target setting, and performance evaluation, looking for fast results and a similar set of KPIs. This would lead to the continuance of the current Box approach that may not fit a future set of innovations or new businesses.

Forgetting

When a new business is planned to emerge out of innovation or as a strategy to continue growth patterns in a new set of segments, the company CEO is expected to address the following about NEW businesses to get out of being entrenched deeply.

- Business planning template that needs a change
- Forecasting mechanism and accuracy
- Predictability of business cycle
- Customer expectations or pattern of customer demands
- Skill sets or competencies to let go off
- Target setting and performance review parameters
- Organizational design
- Business communication approach with customers and internal stakeholders
- Reward mechanism in the current set-up
- Talent hiring policies and processes to be forgotten
- Deeply ingrained mindset and culture to transition to new
- Changing behaviors
- History of successes that no longer the support future
- Creating isolation between the current set-up and NEW, which is a contradictory and challenging one, too, as we understand this more in the next steps!

The above "Forgetting" steps are triggered and executed by hiring key management roles from outside the current set-up, especially ones that head the NEW business functions. Outsiders would challenge organizational culture and mindset that do not support the NEW.

Reconsider communication policies and modes, and review established modes of inter-departmental communications, those that may not be compatible with the NEW (e.g., Sales, Marketing, corporate communications, etc.).

Question the relevance of performance KPIs and also its alignment with customer success factors for NEW. Hanging on to the current set of performance parameters may reinforce current execution methods for success.

Of course, measure the performance of NEW business leadership based on objective and strategic, incremental progress than just revenue and achievement of just revenue, profitability related business plans. Look out and set KPIs (or lead measures) for long-term results.

Borrowing

While we discussed isolating the current set-up from the NEW, it needs a pragmatic view since such isolation is impossible, thus making NEW one have scant resources to perform. Enterprises delivering great in the current set-up carry significant brand values, manufacturing or plant capabilities, great sales connections with customers, purchasing process, enterprise systems, accounting methodologies, etc.

This step would call for a measured approach that drives out too much borrowing, which may result in duplicity or embracing the same structure and, at the same time, investing all efforts in leveraging key assets like brand, and manufacturing, some of the key talents from current set-up.

To keep borrowing is easy and accountable without putting too much burden on the current setup - you need to have a well-established communication link among senior leadership teams on both sides. Resources need the right recognition and create an aspired career path in the right direction. Borrowing resources or plant capacities should yield motivating results versus external customers to keep an interest in supporting the NEW setup.

Consider the successful leveraging of Bosch Gmbh as a great enterprise. Bosch Rexroth, the Industry arm of Bosch Gmbh, leverages the brand image of Bosch, its manufacturing processes, and customer connections from core sectors to ensure other businesses too to be successful.

Indian business conglomerate TATA efficiently leverages its business brand and best practices across the customer spectrum for success, starting from Automotive, House-holds, consumer segments, and Information Technologies (IT) delivery services, which at the same time maintains enough isolations, and balanced integrations.

Amazon, a book-selling company diversifying its portfolio, is another great example of leveraging its brand value.

Netflix innovating its strategy, which started as a DVD rental company, forayed into live streaming, leveraging internet technology and its brand in the entertainment industry. The rest is history.

When borrowing happens, there is a risk of conflict between the current and new business units. This can happen if the current customers are not well served, there are competing preferences for resource allocation, or if the new venture risks damaging the company's brand image or values. There is also a risk of the new technology or business model taking away all the current customers and harming the revenue of the current business.

"Borrowing" resources from one business unit to another can be successful if it is balanced and only includes elements that are unique and supportive to both the current and new ventures. This can be facilitated by shared cultural values and a structured approach. To minimize conflict, it is important to have the right incentives and compensation in place for the shared resources.

Collaborative systems and active management supervision can help reduce tensions between the current and new ventures. It is also important to manage any potential resentment or friction within the current organization through tactical alignment among leadership teams.

This approach also helps to ensure that tensions do not disrupt or destroy the current assets.

Learning

In business, new ventures need to learn quickly about the unknown, uncertainties, business models, customer expectations, and experiences. This enables them to be successful and more predictable.

New businesses usually start with a set of assumptions that need to be tested quickly to ensure the success or failure of the new venture at a lower cost and faster pace.

Learning to predict business outcomes faster and faster, better and better over time, leads to better estimates and, finally, business forecasts leading to better business planning and management.

Analyzing deviations from predictions and determining potential corrective measures can provide valuable learning for establishing a new venture. Staying flexible and adapting to changing circumstances rather than following rigid predictions will help the new venture succeed in the long term. This will also allow organizations to make informed decisions and stay in business. This is to ensure the rule of *"When to HOLD and when to FOLD"* isn't applied in haste.

The core message is to be successful with strategy as a key lever for innovation and manage the three boxes effectively and efficiently. This is achieved by forgetting, borrowing, and learning actions as key capabilities, not just by great visions.

"If your actions inspire others to dream more, learn more, do more, and become more, you are a leader."

~John Quincy Adams

"My job is not to be easy on people. My job is to take these great people we have and to push them and make them even better."

– Steve Jobs

The big pharmaceutical giant called Pfizer transformed its innovation program into a corporate strategy that helps develop new products and increase employee engagement. Now, 80% of the company's employees participate in more than 200 innovation projects. The company has announced nine award programs, which have built a knowledge base of more than 1000 innovation stories.

This is a clear indicator of how an organization can leverage a personal strategy that inspires the individual, finally promoting growth for both employees and the company. This strategy should be inspiring, motivating, challenging, memorable, and unique and should provide a clear vision of the future direction of the business. It can help lead people into a brighter future.

Note that Strategizing is not just a logical process; it is also a creative one. One of the interesting aspects of strategy development is that it requires creativity. While you can use pre-made strategies, it is also important to be able to create and customize strategies and continuously invent new approaches that fit your specific situation.

Managing The Resources While Developing Innovation Strategies -

- **Economic Scale:** It is important to manage the initial funds that bring the first level of strategy for your business. Lower the cost of your goods/services while remaining innovative. Offer unique features and high-quality customer service. For example, Walmart always tries to sell its products at a much lower price, increasing its sales through a large customer base and generating higher profits.

- **Three Fold Alignment:** Barclays Bank was subjected to strong criticism from governance and risky behaviour that contributed to the 2008 financial crisis. A series of scandals, such as foreign exchange fixing, came out. A report commissioned by Barclays in 2013 revealed a corporate culture that wasn't fit for the purpose, tending to "favour transactions over relationships, short term over sustainability, and financial over other business purposes." It further revealed that the fertile environment of the bank had become rather reckless and risky.

Companies that score highly on purpose but low on strategy may manifest poor customer attraction and retention, higher-than-expected costs, organizational dysfunctions, or simple financial underperformance. Instead, businesses need to have a strong threefold alignment between their ***strategy, organization, and purpose.***

> *"However beautiful the strategy, you should occasionally look at the results."*
>
> **~Winston Churchill**

- **Time to market:** Carefully evaluate the options of "build versus buy" for the products/services that you plan to offer your customers. Sometimes, it might be

cheaper to buy part of the products or solutions that are already available or outsource to a third-party vendor to save some cost of producing your goods/services and getting them out in the market.

- **Time to introspect:** An innovative strategy encourages businesses to introspect. It offers a guide on how your business is performing internally and externally. Businesses that can identify their strengths and weaknesses understand themselves better. This is crucial for gaining a competitive advantage and securing future profitability. You may also implement SWOT Analysis or other operational tactics to manage your time and resources efficiently.

You see, we may use the word "strategy" to describe so many different ideas in our personal and professional life. Whether it is a plan for a business or a personal approach to solving a challenge, an "effective innovative strategy" can help your business and life grow in a positive direction that may not have been possible without it.

Summary

While having innovation as a core element in business planning takes centre stage, the right strategy itself acts as an innovation for an organization. While organizations continue to enjoy the current business successes, they find it hard to redeploy resources to new areas which are risky, having long terms to mature and offer returns on Investment.

Clear emphasis is made to focus on future business needs while continuing to focus on execution and optimizing the efficiency of current business, also the most important aspect of forgetting some aspects while creating a new set of businesses beyond the current core.

As an entrepreneur, you may encounter failures on the innovation journey. However, failing early and learning from failures makes further strategies stronger.

Finally, a strategy needs overall alignment across functions and accountability and disciplined execution.

Unboxing Innovation – Rules for Using Your Strategic Resources

Organization and Resource management to unleash Innovation

Innovation as a key strategic lever: we understood how this could be leveraged for survival and thriving even during challenging times of a VUCA world. While a strategy is being worked out for driving innovation, it is important that organizational set-up and resource alignment to drive the innovation are aligned.

The recent pandemic COVID-19 impacted every aspect of our personal life (how we live, work, engage socially, travel, etc.) and professional life (how companies engage with customers and vendors, how goods are delivered through the supply chain, equipment start-ups and commissioning, service supports, etc.)

In a recent survey by a consulting firm (McKinsey & Company, 2020), the executive survey brought out interesting aspects of post-COVID-19. Some of the key messages are as below -

- Although most executives feel innovation is most critical, very few feel that they are equipped to face the challenges

- 90% believe that COVID-19 will change the way we do business over the next 5 years

- 85% are concerned that their customer's needs and wants will change in the next 5 years

- About 21% have the resources and commitment to pursue new growth successfully

- About 2/3rd believe that this will be the most challenging moment in their executive career

- The priority for innovation had dropped from 55% Pre-COVID level to 23%, a significant drop of 32% points, indicating organizations are focusing on the present. Specifically, organizations are focusing on shoring up their core business, pursuing known opportunity spaces, conserving cash, and minimizing risks.

However, in the particular time of crisis, it is advised to focus on the following key focus area-

a. Adapting core to shifting customer needs

b. Identifying and addressing new opportunities opened by the changing landscape

c. Revisiting the innovation portfolio and allocating the right resources appropriately

d. Building a foundation for post-crisis (new norm) to maintain the growth trajectory being competitive and differentiated.

Historically, during and post-crisis, companies that stayed invested in innovation have benefited a lot more than others in revenue and profitability. e.g., during 2009, innovative companies delivered more than 30% profits vs the market average and continued to outperform for the next 3 to 5 years.

Guideposts for Innovation execution for NEW businesses-

- Discover weak signals and non-linear shifts around business

- Identify non-customers and fence-sitting customers who are ready to jump the ship on either side

- Innovation Portfolio thinking: Choose ideas that serve market needs, create new markets, variety of innovation projects around, and balance risk levels.

- Ability to Learn quickly, fail cheaply, fail early

- Resource Mobilization

- Evolve new business models beyond technological innovations

- Conflict mitigation between Core business and NEW business regarding core assets leverage

- Reverse Innovation, taking innovation results to developed nations as is or with little modifications

- Accelerate: Start with a smaller bet as an effective way to manage risks

Strategic Resources

What are strategic resources? The brand name of the current core, Plant and machinery, current sales network, and a team of competent people cutting across the present core and NEW business needs are the most valuable resources for the continuity of the current core business and NEW innovation.

Building a dedicated team for NEW

It is highly recommended to consider the following key elements when building a dedicated team for innovation to create a NEW business or segment out of innovation.

- **Innovation as continuity:** Great breakthroughs are never finished but continue surpassing their own creations and successes into better ones.

- **Openness to outside ideas and skills:** The Innovative set-up welcomes ideas across spectrums with curiosity, openness to review, and embrace the ones that fit the innovation journey.

- **Eagerness to challenging endeavours:** Innovation is also like an expedition that requires enough tenacity and resilience built inside the team. This is like building muscles over years of regular exercising tenure. A mindset to eagerly get into innovation expeditions makes it successful.

- **Experimentation:** Innovation and creating a NEW business involve a great depth of critical assumptions. Willingness to experiment, test the hypothesis of assumptions, learn, adapt learning into the innovation journey, and do trials again and again to achieve desired results make innovation efforts greatly successful. Such an experimentation mindset over a long tenure strongly cements an innovation set-up.

- **Alternative plans:** Innovation efforts and expected results carry high risks and unknowns. In the event of larger deviations versus expectations, a set of alternate plans to continue creating future NEW is necessary across the organization, specifically in teams.

- **Beyond dominant logic:** This relates to the main means a company uses to make a profit. In essence, it is an interpretation of how a company has succeeded. It describes the cultural norms and beliefs that the company espouses. Dedicated teams need to have competencies to generate and execute ideas out of nonlinear shifts and, most importantly, to be free from dominant logic, structures and practices prevailing around.

- **Resource allocation:** Resource allocation is carried out based on the attractiveness of innovation efforts and sustained financial investments, well protected to ensure that funds are not invested back into the current core business. To the greatest extent possible, distinctly identify the skill sets that will be required to create a

NEW future. Also, identify skill sets existing in-house in order to decide whether to borrow from the current set-up or so-called performance engine or to hire from external sources.

While identifying skill sets, be specific as much as possible instead of using terms like "Technical expertise".

Insulate teams of the current core and NEW, but offer enough freedom for a NEW setup to draw necessary, competent resources for creating the future. The crew constantly senses change as the NEW future is being built.

When critical assets are borrowed from the current core setup, evaluate potential conflicts and a mitigation plan. For e.g., the current core may not be willing to share engineering resources or may be concerned with the usage of the same brand (logo, etc.) with a potential threat and may be concerned about cannibalization when a new innovation starts influencing current customers. So, to maintain healthy borrowing between the current core and NEW business, establish robust dialogues and nurture open communication.

Critical assets being planned for borrowing from the current core should be so compelling (clear competitive advantage) that it can make or break success out of innovation.

The Innovation journey encompasses transformation from chaos (multiple orders, looks like chaos from a distance) existing in an organization to perceived stability. It's a cyclic movement just before another cycle of innovation begins.

Execution of Innovation at tactical levels

The strategic alignment of overall organizational goals and innovations is one part of the innovation journey. Further, taking these innovation messages across and translating strategic goals into tactical execution actions needs with granular detailing.

Environment for Innovation

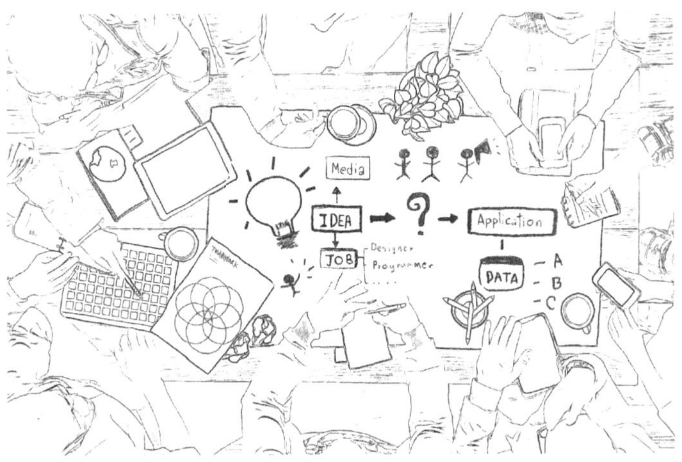

- A clear message from management across functions about the critical dependency of innovation elements and organizational goals of innovation

- Openness in the departments and at all hierarchies about innovation also as an experimental element, tolerance to failure and learning

- Linking career growth in specific target functions to contributions to innovation

- Creating a culture across employees for having an outward outlook for a market pulse, customer needs, technological shifts etc., rather than inward looking. Encourage embracing external inputs in the innovation journey

- Diverse performance parameter for teams involved in innovation projects

- Employees having ease of access to knowledge sources.

- Exposure of innovation team members to pan-industry events on the latest developments, technological shifts, and focus training, inviting special lecture series on innovation from industry leaders bringing academia and industry to exchange best practices. Etc.

- Rewarding innovators beyond financial terms like recognitions, celebrations, rejuvenation and delegation of authority of appropriate levels to enable the innovation journey.

- Enriching a physical workplace conducive to creativity and innovation with the right ergonomics, positive setup and supporting infrastructure covering both physical and information technology. E.g., Creative names like war rooms, names of famous innovators, whiteboards, digital boards, etc.

- Reduce or eliminate the interference of bureaucracy by offering the right delegation of authority for decisions.

- Executive patrons (high-positioned managers) or innovators to keep them as go-to-point to support beyond hierarchies.

- Involvement in Innovation - leadership team needs to offer sufficient bandwidth to actively engage in innovation activities at appropriate levels. Leadership may offer an exciting, diverse idea or solution to a sticky situation and also send a clear message to the innovation team about commitments.

Talent acquisition (Hiring)-

- Have a structured hiring process and selection parameters suitable for innovation jobs

- Get candidates of diverse backgrounds - gender, region, language, functional areas (need be tech areas only)

- Having expertise in two fields, one of which is a core, and going beyond that.

- Enjoy doing innovation work

- Highly collaborative in nature, most of the time individual contributors.

- Problem-solving orientation, resilient to failures, tenacity to focus on achieving end results

- Ability to bring different ways of looking and diverse perspectives to issues.

- Willingness to cross-collaborate with customers, vendors and internal stakeholders

The above elements shall be a part of job descriptions, screening, interviewing and final selection processes.

In summary, while the right strategy for innovation is a MUST, however having the right organizational setup, resource management, and execution are recipes to make an innovation journey a successful one.

Summary

Innovation being leveraged as a strong lever, greater emphasis is needed on resources, reinforcing organizational set-up and environment conducive for strong innovation deliveries. With a fast-changing business environment, the situation calls for an agile organizational setup to respond to the market. An organizational environment that embraces openness to new ideas, failure tolerance, open to experimentation, and the ability to learn from failures motivates innovation among teams.

The human resources in the current core need to be selectively drawn into creating a future NEW business beyond the current core. This calls for a pragmatic and differentiated way of compensation, hiring, rewarding and career progression policies, and a different set of goals in the beginning. This all starts with a talent acquisition strategy focusing on the right job descriptions, competency needs and selection processes, and well-aligned deliverables at different stages of business progression in contrast to the existing core focused on operational efficiency, profitability, etc.

Chapter IV

Survive Today & Thrive Tomorrow – Crafting Winning Strategies out of the RED Ocean

We are probably going through one of the most significant historical changes in the last 100 years. Old businesses are changing, and New businesses are emerging. We are already seeing a shift in innovation technologies, as discussed in previous chapters, at a higher pace than before. Organizations today have become more vigilant and cautious, especially in the post-COVID era, with new norms for working.

In the previous chapter, we understood about leveraging strategy itself as an innovation lever to address market needs, create new markets and continue to grow in a disruptive, competitive economy.

"Our industry does not respect tradition.
It only respects innovation."

~Satya Nadella, CEO of Microsoft

Now, let us understand how an Innovation strategy needs to be embraced to make the innovation journey a successful one.

Innovative ideas are accompanied by the following key essentials as we embark on an execution mode-

- Brief about the industry that the idea is targeting to address and also brief about the idea itself

- What differentiates this idea as a radical one or disruptive technology or disruptive model? Reassure yourself that this is not merely an incremental innovation in the current business.

- What market signals or non-linear shifts in the economy are connected with this new idea

- What customer pain points are being addressed, or are you planning to address

- Target pricing to address customer needs

- Does the idea have a high chance of feasibility and also a high level of attractiveness (address unmet customer needs, converting non-customers as customers, affordable, profitable, market size at target pricing, etc.)

- What are the values created for customers

- What is the business model and value creation structure for customers from ideation to the final product or service delivery at the customer end?

- What capabilities are required, core competencies to be developed, to be hired from outside, to be licensed, etc.

- Critical assumptions made and testing those assumptions or hypotheses for potential risks or assumed gains

While we are working on thriving in a highly competitive or over-fished red ocean, let us consider some of the approaches though there could be some overlapping similarities.

In this chapter, we cover some of the tools or strategies that we may adopt in driving our innovation strategies and supporting long-term growth.

TOTO Matrix Approach

This is adopted in its original form from *"How to thrive in Chaos." –Dr. Nadya Zexembayeva*, from the Reinvention Academy, one of my inspirational coaches on Reinvention.

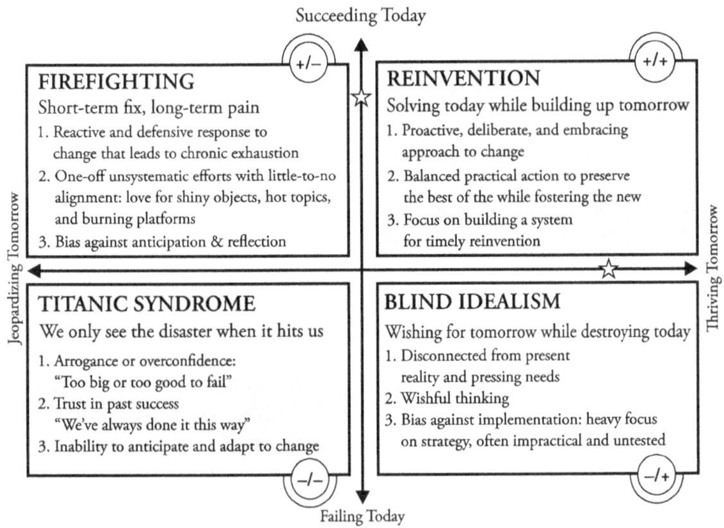

TOTO refers to Today and Tomorrow and is apt for today's highly dynamic VUCA economic world. The TOTO matrix

represents different growth and survival scenarios based on the actions and approaches of enterprises.

Blind Idealism: This quadrant is characterised by wishing for tomorrow while destroying or a downfall today. The executives are entrenched with wishful thinking bias against the implementation of change needs, highly focused on untested strategy formulations, and less on executions. Organisations are disconnected from present pressing needs and realities. The chances are that they may grow tomorrow at the cost of today, but with an uncertain future, since investments for tomorrow are from today's earnings.

Fire-fighting: The activities are diametrically opposite to blind idealism. The organisation is always in a reactive and defensive response to market needs or change needs, leading to exhaustion. Very little alignment on the system approach for performance focus and love for short-term fixings, leading to long-term pains. There will be a large bias against anticipation and reflection in the organisation. The organisation ends up struggling to survive today, having low chances for tomorrow's needs and expectations of the ecosystem, jeopardising tomorrow.

Titanic Syndrome: As briefed in the other chapter, Titanic syndrome is a corporate disease that makes one believe that they are mighty, too big and strong to fail as an organisation and carry the arrogance or overconfidence of past successes that could make them strive for longer. Strong belief in "we have always done like this", and it will work. Such a scenario is characterised by an inability to anticipate and adapt to change.

Reinvention: Organisations and executives are deliberate and proactive and embrace an approach to change. The company has a Pragmatic approach towards transitioning to the new while retaining the core that works for the future too. The enterprise has systems to anticipate change and design and implement changes in a timely manner.

In order to have an innovation successful and a continual growth curve strategically, having a Reinvention mindset and Reinvention culture at every part of the strategy is a boon to the organisation for surviving both today and tomorrow. This quadrant is a classic example of how an organisation can transition to new S-curves of growth with constant reinvention initiatives. A constant endeavour to push the (star) marks on X and Y coordinates in positive directions in this quadrant enhances the level of success for today and tomorrow.

Blue ocean strategy for successful innovation

The market in every aspect and every walk of life is filled with intense competition fighting for their pie out of the available market, pushing the prices down, ever-ending price war, mergers and acquisitions and many enterprises in constant survival mode. In the red ocean scenario, players keep their focus on beating competition within the existing market, exploiting existing market demands.

The concept of the Blue ocean strategy was introduced through a book published by W. Chan Kim in 1994.

It is based on the view that market boundaries and industry structures are *not given* and can be *reconstructed* by the actions and beliefs of industry players. The strategy is based on creating an *uncontested* marketplace, thereby making the *competition irrelevant*. The offerings to customers are based on differentiation, lower cost to open new market space and create new demand.

While Innovations are technology-driven, market-pioneering and futuristic, Blue Ocean aligns innovation with utility, price and cost positions for sustained growth while at the same time creating market spaces.

The following table simplifies the fundamental difference between Red ocean and Blue ocean strategies.

Red Ocean Strategy	Blue Ocean Strategy
Compete in Existing market Place	Create new uncontested market place
Beat the competition	Making the competition Irrelevant
Exploiting existing demand	Create, capture New demand
Based on Value-Cost trade-off	Breaking Value-cost trade-off
Aligning organisational strategic choices based on Differentiation or lower cost approach (cost leader or feature leader)	Aligning organisational strategic choices based on Differentiation AND lower cost approach (Differentiation at competitive price)

Reference: Chan Kim & Renée Mauborgne. Blue Ocean Strategy

Value Innovation: Blue Ocean strategy's most impactful framework to grow market share and succeed in entrepreneurship while minimising risks is value creation, represented below. The framework asks the four most important questions to create new market space and a high marginal value to customers.

What should be Reduced? Which factors should be *reduced* well above the industry standard?	What should be Raised? Which factors should be *raised* well above the industry standard?
What should be Eliminated? Which factors that the industry had long competed on be *eliminated?*	What should be created? Which factors should be *created* that the industry had never offered?

Consider the innovation already on hand or look at the current portfolio of products, solutions or services on-hand and apply the above questioning techniques to assess and work further.

To simplify, review multiple times and seek feedback from peers or experts, and number each of those answers at each quadrant or post-it on a wall to pick the best of choices and enhance further. You get more room to think over these Q&A deliberations for enrichment.

To drive Innovation with leverage of strategy execution, we do not need great visionaries or minds but simply following approaches-

- *Review* the industry, identify customer needs they are served and also not served

- Study the industry's customers and non-customers for what they need

- *Restructure* the offering by focusing on customer needs, eliminating those that don't serve the needs.

How will a leader respond in today's scenario?

- A leader needs to set challenging goals, analyse data quickly and create a culture of doing everything smarter, cheaper and faster. A leader needs to understand and differentiate the various stages of the company, at the same time differentiating the product from its rivals. There may be a high risk of customer rejection in today's times as the choices are abundant. Therefore, the company must keep moving its business strategy dynamically.

Current Transition

We are currently transitioning into a time where there is an immense ability to build a greater future. Many innovators across the globe are creating space and building structures for new non-linear ideas. Young minds are willing to let go of past practices, habits, activities and attitudes.

A leader needs to establish a formal regime (which also involves gathering and analysing weak signals), champion the idea of maverick thinkers, set an example for the company by sidelining foot draggers, and anticipate the needs of experimenters and thinkers.

The current scenario sometimes requires us to move away from the traditional hierarchal models of decision-making in

order to make decisions that better reflect the market needs and allow real-time adaptation.

It is not easy to state in a few words what the current leader must do, but there are some components that are mandatory to determine success.

The crude form of leadership used to rely solely on a single form of satisfaction called monetary rewards. However, today, the rewards are more metaphorical than literal. Employees today respond to love, prestige, career plans, independence, achievement, group membership, new discoveries, and relationships with others.

In other words, human beings respond not only to the traditional carrot and stick used by the driver of the donkey. They also respond to ambition, patriotism, love of good, beauty, boredom, self-doubt, encouragement and many more dimensions of thoughts and feelings that make them human beings.

Future

What has the future in store for us?

The future is clear and understood from simple perspectives. Any business enterprise will build a nonlinear future mainly by experimentation that tests assumptions and resolves uncertainties. Hedging risks and bringing new learnings will either strengthen the idea or reveal its weaknesses.

The only challenge over here is - If the innovator develops many new ideas, it is not always obvious which idea to pursue first. So we would require a method to gauge relative value and priority. So that knowing the success rate becomes easy.

To sum it up, no decision is worth the name unless it involves balancing risks and returns. Mistakes are inevitable. But our executive's concern should be to watch over long-term growth.

How will a leader facilitate a growing future?

"It's not the strongest species that survive, nor the most intelligent, but the most responsive to change."

~Charles Darwin

A leader's efforts do not go only on revenue generation, But rather also on the quality and pace of learning from experiments. Whether it is the pharmaceutical industry, financial services, product designing, telecommunications, construction companies, hospitals, NASA, or any other, organisations learn from their failures to improve the future. In some cases, non-linear ideas are launched into embryonic markets just to test assumptions. Therefore, organisations need to effectively detect and analyse failures instead of repeating a self-serving statement such as *"markets were not ready for our great new product"*.

Every child, at some point, learns from admitting their failures and taking responsibility for them. Hence many organisations have shifted to a culture of psychological safety in which the reward of learning from failure can be fully realized.

A Leader can create and reinforce a culture that counteracts the negative factors and instead proactively searches for opportunities to experiment.

"Risk management is a more realistic term than safety. It implies that hazards are ever-present, that they must be identified, analyzed, evaluated and controlled or rationally accepted."

~Jerome F. Lederer

If Covid-19 Pandemic has taught us one thing, it is that there are far too many risks simply off the organization's radar. Companies need to create a well-defined, intelligent support system that establishes a framework for operational risk.

Risk managers need to analyse captured information, sense their organisation's reporting line, understand on-screen and off-screen communication, and report the status to key stakeholders.

Given early recognition, specific management actions, tasks, and controls can be defined to mitigate, reduce or eliminate risks while enabling corporations to profitably utilise any opportunity normally accompanied by these risks.

Summary

In today's VUCA world; the Key message is about focusing on quadrant one for organisations to succeed today as well as thrive tomorrow with clearly crafted innovation and execution strategies, not to be drawn into the Titanic syndrome.

Blue Ocean's strategy is to create uncontested space outside of Red Ocean, making the competition irrelevant, focusing on value creation, creating and capturing new markets, and strong facilitation from leadership to navigate.

PART IV

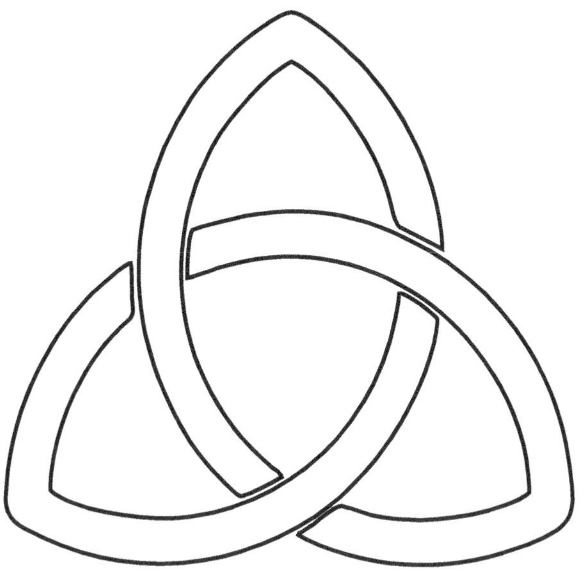

Design Thinking – Bringing Customers to the Centre of Core

The apartment complex where I have been staying for the past decade has witnessed a transition from having all its administrative functions performed manually to an efficient, hi-tech digitalization of operations. Thanks to advances in technology that have made this possible in recent years.

Let's look at what the scenario was in the initial years. Whenever a resident had a visitor or a parcel delivery person, the main gate security had to call on that particular resident's landline number and inform them. There are 228 apartments in the complex. Imagine the endless calls security personnel had to make throughout the day. Moreover, it was quite annoying for us residents as well, getting 4-5 calls per day. Some residents made requests, telling them," Please do not call, we get disturbed ! Why don't you just send the person inside" was answered with", we are not allowed to do that, we have to adhere to security protocol".

This is one example. Similarly, there were many more instances of making tasks difficult. Previously, any intimation for residents or information sharing had to be communicated through the notice board, where typed notices had to be put manually in each block. Now all that is done through the app only. Here's a perfect example of design thinking in action: a genuine human need that leads to idea generation and technological possibilities worthy of business success. The Managing Committee, which is the governing body of the apartment, comprising a group of volunteer residents, discussed many options, brainstormed with the residents, weighed the pros/cons, and finally decided to digitalize the process through an app.

Hence, a need to solve a problem led to idea generation and implementation of the best solution. Of course, this involved some degrees of risk-taking and tolerance for failure. A group of residents were selected for the trial and testing before finalizing. In the initial stages, loopholes were there – residents who weren't very tech savvy found using the app bit difficult, sometimes people didn't receive notifications, and so on. Ultimately, these were sorted out, and the end result was a user-friendly, multi-purpose app where you could do so much with the touch of a button, saving time and energy and making the processes so efficient.

Chapter I

Introduction to Design Thinking – What is the Framework to Start with?

Design Thinking

In Part-I, titled CREATIVITY, we understood more about creativity as relevant to business and how a culture of creativity can be inculcated in organizations and also individually.

We also realized creativity is not that it's innate for very few by birth but can be harvested by every human being through efforts and adopting certain ways and tools. Creativity is the beginning of all innovations, successful entrepreneurship and further making those innovations is widely adopted by the public at large, not just a "creation" limited to labs.

In this part, focused on Design Thinking, you would understand the concept of Design Thinking, how to identify customer or user needs, the idea generation process to solve identified challenges, how to identify and pick customer implicit needs by going through a deep customer immersion journey, creating alternate solutions, prototyping, building and presenting a business case and commercialization. Further, most important, you shall also get to know briefly how we consider environmental aspects while bringing innovation to the fore.

A famous Design thinker Arne van Oosterom said aptly; ***"Design Thinking is a mindset, not a tool kit or series of steps."***

Introduction to Design Thinking

When we think of a Designer, what comes to mind is someone who roles out a product, goes through iterations to achieve desired outcomes (prototyping), and finally, with fine aesthetics for the user. Applying this principle of Design, collectively known as "Design Thinking", at various steps, throughout the product life cycle and the way people work, is becoming the core of many successful enterprises.

With fast-evolving technological disruptions and market volatilities, the business environment becomes more and more complex; Software takes centre stage over Hardware many times, enhancing the complexity of system integrations, addressing customer needs, and also the necessity of addressing faster time-to-market. Every enterprise is constantly challenged with users looking for an experience of Simple, Intuitive, and Delightful experiences out of products and services. In the services areas, rolling out a user-centric solution makes it more challenging with a fragmented approach.

In principle, Design Thinking instils Customer Empathy, adopting Prototyping Principle, and a tolerance for failure at an early stage (a rather cheap failure) in creating solutions. This widely adopted principle across enterprises promotes a flexible, responsive organizational culture with a user focus. Design thinking is multifaceted, cross-functional approach to help people bring innovative ideas to life.

Design Thinking, at first, used to be closely related and applied to the delivery of physical objects. However, it found widespread adaptation into complex systems like customer experiences as services.

An important element of the Design Thinking approach is the incorporation of customers' emotional needs, which can be explicit or implied needs derived from the customer empathy journey (detailed in further chapters). Many products and solutions delivered with this approach have a strong emotional connection and are simpler in nature, even with some features removed with a deliberate attempt focused on what a product should "not do". Emotions that are normally associated with the launch of a product or service are aspirations, desires, engagements, and experiences.

Failure Tolerant culture is another key attribute of Design Thinking since Design involves iterative processes (prototyping) that may not yield success at first instances.

"Ultimate Driving Machine" is the emotional phrase that explains BMW's automobile wizardry. The phrase was coined in the 1970s to attract customers and consistently connect with emotions who enjoy driving.

"The Best or Nothing" slogan from Mercedes-Benz embodies the quality of vehicles the brand provides and its intents ingrained in every function in the organization.

Frame work of Design Thinking

As we step into understanding more about the framework, let's recap how it starts!

When imagination is applied to visualize something that doesn't exist, the outcome leads to creativity. Creativity leads to Innovation, and further successful commercialization leads to entrepreneurship.

> *"Design thinking is a human-centred approach to innovation that draws from the designer's toolkit to integrate the needs of people, the possibilities of technology, and the requirements for business success."*
>
> **~Tim Brown, Executive chair of IDEO**

Design Thinking, in the exact words of IDEO (Global Design and Innovation Company), is an intersection of "Desirability", "Feasibility", and "Viability".

IDEO is often credited with the pioneering term "Design Thinking" and its practice. Design thinking strongly encapsulates empathy, iterative process, optimism, creative confidence, experimentation, and embracing ambiguity and failure.

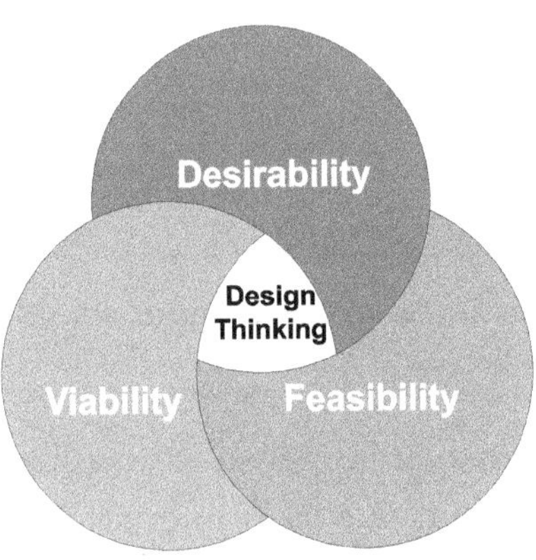

Let's start with the "Desirability" aspect of the framework; it's about people looking for a solution to a challenge on-hand. This is linked to a stated need or latent need that the customer (people) is looking for to be addressed by way of an appropriate solution, and the customer is willing to pay for it. This desirability also applies to addressing some of the "unmet" desires of the customer in current products or services.

The next element of the framework is the "Feasibility" aspect that we have a "Technically" feasible solution possible for the issue being addressed. It doesn't necessarily mean we solve all technical solutions in one go, but a directionally correct "feasible" solution is the right step. A feasible solution is capable of meeting the customer's (user) needs in the specified environment at all times.

The "Viability" element is related to the fact that, though technically feasible; is it affordable to a larger set of target users? Can the solution be made available on a sustained basis on commercial viability?

In another way, Design Thinking is also explained as an intersection of "REAL" (The problem we intend to address is a real one), WIN (solutions that we offer solve customer issues as desired) and WORTH (means the solutions developed are worthy of being in business on a sustained basis)

In summary, the success of all these three elements contributes to the success of an innovation.

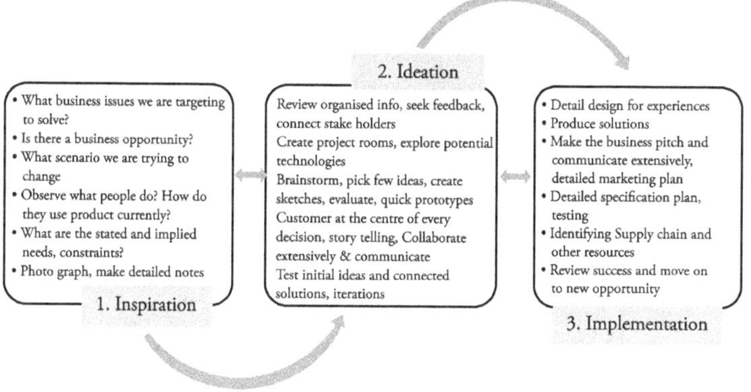

As we know by this time, Design thinking embraces ambiguity and tolerance to failures. Hence, we need to start with all the elements together to succeed, but we may begin with the people dimension or our core strength and expertise to address challenges. However, eventually need to address all these three elements to arrive at a successful innovation.

A few successful innovations that had immense user focus and deep customer immersion are listed below:

Gillette brand razor (P&G portfolio): The acquisition of Gillette by P&G in 2005 offered a great opportunity for P&G

since both Gillette and P&G were successful brands. The need was to successfully leverage strategic capabilities and create new ones where capabilities did not exist to the extent required to win. Gillette needed to have specific capabilities to address the needs of the men's grooming segment of shaving in India. This, in turn, would need P&G's deep customer understanding and leading innovation into play. P&G's deep-dive ethnographic approach to customer research was an asset and something new for Gillette, which had previously relied on standard quantitative research. The chronology that followed in rolling out a new razor is fascinating, and the sequence is depicted below:

- Chip Bergh, President of the men's grooming business, also oversaw the integration of Gillette into P&G

- One of the strategic priorities for Gillette was to expand in emerging markets, specifically India.

- Bergh called upon the team to think differently about addressing consumers in emerging markets like India, and a meeting was scheduled.

- A session; the first ever "Design-from-scratch" innovation for an emerging market with leading Scientists from the UK, and Boston, marketing people, and market-research people.

- Bergh's direction to the team was simple "the first thing is to spend two weeks in India, live with these consumers, visit their homes, understand how they shave and how shaving fits into their lives."

- There were surprising responses and suggestions to get the local Indian populace on board around the vicinity and understand. But Bergh was clear with his experience in engaging with customers in India, on the ground, in the actual Indian market.

- Finally, experts visited India, spent days and time with consumers, shopping with them, going to the barber shop with the consumers and watching them shave. It was quite contrary to the remote assumption of the shaving system that Indian consumers go through. Typically razors are designed and tested with the assumption that everyone shaves similar to people in the west, with reliable access to a large sink and running hot water!

- Though the reality observed by team members was that Indian consumers shaved with only a small cup of cold water, which caused small hairs to clog, making it far more difficult to shave.

- Gillette's new shaving product took care of this input, and a new Razor and single-blade system was designed to make it easy-to-use and easy to rinse the cartridge

- By directly engaging with Indian consumers, treating consumers as the boss, understanding difficulties and finally relating to the company's mission statement about improving consumers' lives.

(Referenced from the book "Playing to Win" by A.G. Lafley and Roger L Martin, HBR Press)

Orthopaedic aid for polio victims: Dr. Abdul Kalam who pioneered successful missile programs for defence systems in India and is fondly remembered also as "People's President" for his humbleness and care for people. During Kalam's tenure in DRDO (Defense Research and Development Organisation), there was an instance of Dr. Kalam visiting the orthopaedic department at NIMS (Medical Institute) in Hyderabad. There he came across polio-affected boys and girls dragging their feet, assisted by calliper splints made of leather, wood, and steel weighing up to 3-4 kilograms. As an aeronautical engineer who is always looking for opportunities to reduce the weight of flying elements (Rocketry) in order to gain traction efficiently, found an opportunity with these patients to reduce the weights being carried.

With this deep observation and user experience of polio-affected people and the intent to make their living experience better, Dr. Kalam pivoted the DRDO engineers and medical institute orthopaedics to join hands in improving the situation. Within a short span of time, a new orthopaedic appliance FRO (Floor Reaction Orthosis), was developed with advanced, lighter composites to help polio victims stand on their legs. This innovation reduced the weight of 3-4 Kg to merely 300 to 400 Grams.

This is another great example of a user-centric approach to improving life experiences by using Design Thinking mindset of innovation.

The above examples show a particular trend where-in there is clear evidence that customer needs or larger market desires are an essential part of innovation. And, of course, solutions are not derived in one shot but through a process of alternate solutions and iterations, prototyping and trials.

This process of deep understanding of customer needs or customer empathy journey is an important element as a designer contrary to the usual *"I know that the problem is..."* mindset.

Summary

This chapter is an introduction to Design Thinking – the meaning of the term, its significance, and the steps involved throughout the product life cycle. In fact, the entire process by which a product or system is launched is Design thinking!

A prime component of Design Thinking is attention to customer empathy. This goes beyond merely understanding the customer and also having a deeper emotional connection with them. After all, the customer is the King and the King never bargains!

Design Thinking is an all-encompassing, cross-functional approach to assisting people in bringing innovative ideas to life.

Creativity occurs when humans have the ability to imagine and visualize something out of the ordinary!! Such actions entail taking risks, and experimenting and may not always yield immediate results; thus, acceptance of failure is essential.

Desirability, viability, and feasibility are the three main pillars of Design Thinking.

- Desirability is the desire for something, a problem to be solved.

- Viability entails whether the product is affordable and commercially available. Is the problem genuine and worth doing business with?

- Feasibility - can the problem be solved easily and conveniently with the resources and technology available? Or create new technologies to address challenges.

The right blend of these, combined with a series of trial and error, gives rise to innovation.

Chapter II

Opportunity Identification and the Customer Empathy Journey – How to Implement?

In the previous chapters, we understood the principle framework of the Design Thinking process. Three progressive steps starting from Inspiration, then Ideation, and finally implementation, are integrally tied to each other; the Designer at any point gets back to the previous steps to complete the incomplete.

At the organizational level, corporate mission and visions guide the strategies of which product and market segment they would like to play and win or decide *not to play*. Product development strategies start with understanding the real opportunity or customer needs that organizations would like to address and pursue further. Before a project is approved and the actual product development process is, a planning phase gets executed; the output of this planning phase carries details about Opportunity Identification. This phase describes the target market for the product, business goals, key assumptions, and risks too.

*A pictorial view (of the product development process) as adopted from the Product Development Process by Ulrich and Stephen Eppinger. All concept credits and rights of images absolutely belong to those privileged Authors.

Planning	Concept Development	System Level Designs	Detailed Design	Testing and Refinement	Production Ramp-up

Product Development Process

Planning is phase 0 of the entire product development process. This involves alignments with corporate strategies, analysis driving strategic decisions, and the creation of a portfolio of projects to be executed.

At the core of planning, identifying Market Opportunity is an important process apart from Market segmentation, assessing new technologies, consideration for product platforms, and manufacturing-related topics.

In this chapter, we shall dive deep into **How to find Market Opportunities?**

Market opportunity and detailed customer needs identification are very closely interwoven activities. Let's start with Market Opportunity Identification.

In the context of the product development framework, an opportunity is an early trigger for a new product, a sense of opportunity to create value for the user, a potential solution to address a need, applying new technology, or a rough solution for a nonlinear signal from the market to address a need.

For e.g., Asian Paints sensed a chance for a potential in a highly corrosive environment (Like structures at the seashore or sand-storm frequented deserts), a pathology lab seeing an opportunity to address a new emerging pandemic with preventive diagnosis, a need for homecare for a growing population of elderly people in India, an opportunity to process and produce farm products in India that would otherwise perish quickly.

While working on identifying opportunities, specifically in technology areas, it is critical to understand the technology and solutions that are likely to be deployed, as well as the market needs of those likely to absorb the technology and solutions we have available or are developing.

Generally, innovations get deployed with improved technologies where the current customers or markets are not addressed (Adjacent market). Another highly challenging area is looking for a completely new set of customers or market with completely new technologies and a longer horizon from a deployment perspective with high risks-rewards. (Completely new market)

Recommended to have-

a. As many multiple opportunities are generated among teams and individuals

b. Generate as many Quality Ideas as possible

c. Create a set of highly variant, divergent ideas resulting from wild thinking

Having generated all those varieties of ideas, it is essential to go through qualifying methods to have very few sets of ideas as a funnel for opportunities. Further financial analysis, strategic fits, and competition analysis pass through as real opportunities.

What are the sources of opportunity identification?

- **Your Passion:** You are passionate about certain activities and hobbies and want to strive better at them with new technologies, trends, and emerging use cases. These could be a source of inspiration for opportunities.

- **Your own experiences around:** As an individual, most innovators find something out of their own dissatisfactions in the surrounding environment in their daily life. Especially the tasks which give frustration to the level," let's finish this quickly" somehow! Such innovators get into deep immersion to get to know others' experiences too and the annoyances around them.

- **Leveraging Strategic Assets:** These are Valuable, Rare, Inimitable, Non-substitutable

Strategic assets offer a stronger degree of leverage in opportunity identification, those aligned with strategic goals.

One of the studies showed that more than 40% of product opportunities are identified within the organization, and the balance is sourced from Customers, competitive products, universities, distribution partners etc.

Concept Development Process

A graphical representation of the Concept development process shared below contains many front-end processes with collaboration among various functions. Many of the steps may go through iterative processeses to achieve the desired results and return to the point where clarification is sought further.

Identify Customer Needs → Establish Target Specifications → Generate Product concepts → Select Product Concepts → Test Product Concepts → Set final Specs → Plan Downstream Developments

Critical elements relevant to customers are-

- Collecting customer needs
- Identify Lead users

Concept Development Process

The whole concept development process gets detailed validation with competitive benchmarking, financial analysis and validation, and also prototyping analysis as its foundation block, along with the above-shared process steps.

Identifying customer needs: One of the most critical steps to start with, an in-depth detail of this process is explained here.

The intent of this process is to clearly understand customer needs and organize and package them to communicate precisely to product development teams internally. The objective of customer needs identification is also to get to know "Latent needs", which customer customers cannot state explicitly during conversations or the interview process. These are discovered by deep observations by the innovation teams. Additionally, customer needs are classified using a hierarchy, weightage, and all needs combined. *Lead users* are also identified who contribute immensely to the innovation process and who might be performing some tasks in roundabout ways or struggling to complete them. This step helps in identifying unaddressed needs with current offerings as well as in developing potential solutions.

One of the McKinsey polls revealed 84% of global executives reported that Innovation is the most important element for their growth strategies. However, a staggering more than 90% of global executives were dissatisfied with their organizations' performance on Innovation, and outcomes fell far short of ambitious goals.

Today, most companies have plenty of information and insights about customers than before. Thanks to the internet, point of sale information, market trends, data science, etc., data culling happens to get a host of information about products, technology, usage etc., to drive innovation processes flawlessly. It appears as if companies have well-mastered innovation techniques and risk mitigations.

However, still, the success of innovation efforts is much less than ambitions in most cases. It is a matter of concern for every organization on the innovation journey.

One of the great authors on Innovation strategy attributes it to the creation of customer databases which are developed to show correlations. (As adapted from "Competing Against luck" by Christensen, Taddy Hall)

Marketers who collect research data, demographic information or purchasing patterns attempt to correlate them in generic forms with other buyers. In the process, the most important missing elements are what the customer is trying to achieve in the given circumstances. This is termed as the customer's "Job to be done", which drives the purpose behind a buy (to help the job to be done).

Successful innovators work on addressing poorly performed customers' job-to-be-done. This also relates to where customers are performing their jobs in a round-about-way since these are unmet customer needs with the current set of products or solutions. By deeply understanding the customer's job-to-be-done, innovators translate deep understanding into a set of customer needs, design the product, buying experience, and processes, putting them to use in achieving customers' jobs.

Key principles prescribed in addressing job-to-be-done are as below-

- Job is something the user is trying to create as an experience, too, while the task on hand is being done in given circumstances.

- While most product developments consider market surveys, data sets, demography, etc., it is essential to consider customer circumstances than customer characteristics. Focus on the underlying job rather than just a generic need.

- **Focus on unmet needs:** Determine which unmet needs of customers are explicitly visible or implied. Currently, customers may address them in a round-about way or

may not have a solution at all and continue to live with their current level of experiences

- **Look for social and emotional connections beyond just functional needs.** This may even extend to revisiting some functions decisively, but emotional needs are met while the job to be done is addressed. This will also include reviewing what jobs customers intend to avoid e.g., (Having to wait in a long queue and go through the registration process for simple hospital care purposes, which could otherwise be handled by a paramedical professional)

- **Creating the best "overall experience";** To make the customer journey from identification of a specific product or solutions, buying, and experiencing the best emotional and social experiences at all touchpoints during the usage cycle. Such overall experience enablers are embedded into the organizational processes.

- **What obstacles are being removed:** in given circumstances, identify the potential obstacles that the customer would like to be removed in order to get the job-to-be-done executed flawlessly.

Precisely, the Design Thinking approach considers all of the above elements when market or customer needs are documented and shared in the right formats with stakeholders in the product development organization.

- **Customer Need Identification Steps:** Simple steps to complete need identification, including the critical process of finding product use environment and direct

experience working with prospects. This process is an integral part of any product development, as it connects market and product development teams and provides better insights to ensure that customer expectations are fulfilled completely with appropriate, known deliberate trade-offs.

The goals of customer need identification steps are clearly to achieve the following-

- Products and solutions are clearly based on Customer needs

- All categories of needs; like Latent needs and explicit needs, are well captured

- Create product specifications that are well understood by the product development team and are aligned with market needs

- Provide credible, fact-based inputs for creating archives of market needs

- Ensure that critical customer needs are not overlooked for any reason

These steps for identifying customer needs are illustrated below.

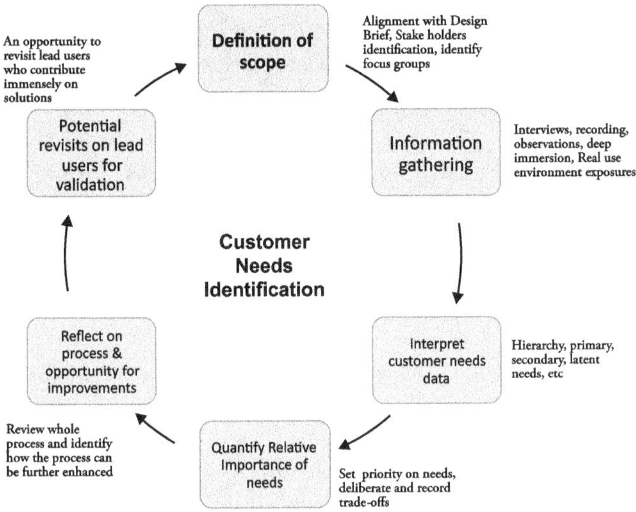

Let's understand some of the important terminologies being used during the needs identification process-

- **Latent Needs:** customer needs which are not yet widely recognized by customers, and the existing products or solutions also do not meet those needs. Customers manage with the current status as it is. Such needs are not expressed specifically by customers, but design teams identify them through deep observations and conversations and extract those needs. Latent needs are also hard to understand just by talking to customers.

  The most important step in achieving customer delight and great user experience is identifying latent needs and exceeding customer expectations.

Once latent needs get integrated into the product development process and become a reality, revealed in the market as successful, such latent needs become "a must-have"; for example, an air conditioner changing temperature by sensing temperature around the sit-out area rather than at the conditioner body itself.

Another classic example is the cover of the coffee cup changing its colour when the temperature reaches comfortable levels for consumers.

- **Primary Needs:** Customer needs expressed or recorded under the generic needs category.

- **Secondary Needs:** Each of the detailed specific needs within the primary group are secondary needs. These will be very specific in nature. Each Primary need may have another 5-10x set of secondary needs.

- **Lead Users:** Lead users are offered experiences ahead of mainstream customers. They become a part of solution creation; products and solutions delivered get additional enrichment if their needs are addressed. This set of users helps in customer needs identification much better and faster.

- **Extreme Users:** This is a group of customers who use products differently and may have special needs. Extreme users contribute to the development of solutions through their own experiences and requirements. For example, a disabled person looking for a wheelchair that can support them in driving through tough terrain in developing countries. Addressing their needs benefits mainstream customers too.

- **Mainstream Customers:** Customers constituting a significant market size and will have common needs as part of products and solutions.

The attached image depicts the Product Innovation Diffusion cycle for reference.

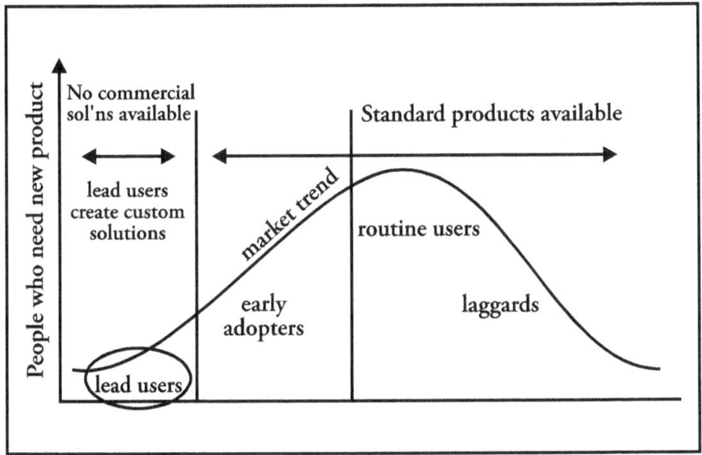

The whole process starts with the project mission statement. Before customer engagement begins on need identification as part of the product development process, a typical mission statement includes the following key elements. Whether it is offering an incrementally different product or a completely radically new offering, it is essential to have directionally suitable offerings in mind. This will set a direction to reach a certain set of customers and markets and target groups for information gathering. In reality, the mission statement would also evolve as the cycle progress.

- Market Opportunity
- Benefits propositions

- Business Goals, Probable target trial and release schedules
- Customers covering both primary market and secondary markets
- Assumptions considered
- Stake Holders (who could be part of that influence or get influenced)

Detailed steps on customer need identifications

1. **Raw data or information Gathering:** As the principle of Design Thinking, the best approach to needs identification is to get information from customers directly firsthand. This is achieved by:

   i. **Interviews:** This is a highly effective option where the target customer is interviewed for about 60-90 mins in free flow, but all aspects were covered with proper preparations in the background. Such interviews are conducted at the customer's premises or in the target use environment.

   ii. **Focus Group Moderations:** Typically, 10-12 customers are grouped in a discussion room where interactions may be observed by team members. These group discussions are moderated by a professional researcher or a member of the product development team. Each of the discussions extends to 2-3 hrs, and sometimes, participants are paid too for participating. The deliberations are noted and recorded in audio/ video formats.

iii. **Deep Observations of "Product-in-use"**– here, the current product in use is closely examined in terms of its usage in the real environment, handling, maintenance and so on. In the absence of a product, tasks are performed in some way where a new product is targeted. These observations can be passive with no interaction or active engagements to collaborate, where team members may also perform target "Job-to-be-done". For example, the P&G product team visited India and spent a couple of days with target customers for in-depth observation, understanding of their routines, purchase behaviour, living environment, how men shaved, etc., in order to develop a Razor set for the Indian market. This provided P&G with deeper insight and a successful product launch in India.

Other data relevant to the target segment may be sourced through secondary market research.

However, as a principle, direct customer feedback is the most preferred in product development in understanding a customer's "job to be done".

From an adequacy point of view, interviews in the range of 15-25 minutes and/or focus group discussions over 3-4 sessions are recommended. Finally, the extent to which customer needs are identified depends on the product segment and spectrum of users. Conclusively it is not about statistical data but rather about clear quantification of customer needs driven by a job-to-be-done approach.

Lead users are recommended to be included as MUST participants since these customers offer deeper insights much ahead of mainstream users or the majority of the market. These Lead users articulate emerging needs better and also have potential solutions because of struggles encountered due to unmet needs.

In the interview process or group moderations, having identified Extreme users (like visually challenged, limited or inadequate literacy, e.g. professional dancers sharing how people fall, factory workers maintaining clean-room inspiring surgeons, the baby carriage being used for grocery loading, etc.) offer special needs. Extreme users are also those who are excluded from the target segment or whose product doesn't meet their intent. Inputs received from extreme users not only benefit them but eventually enhance the user experience of major customer segments.

Tips for effective customer feedback solicitation

- **Active Listening:** Focus on active listening to customers while responding with attention to and acknowledging, paraphrasing customer statements, nodding and other actions that show your interest in the interactions. This motivates customers to engage deeply and move with free-flow conversations. Be alert for surprises; further questioning may lead to interesting revelations.

- **Do not force a solution:** Not to quickly connect with an anticipated product and try to lead the conversation around anticipated solutions.

- **Observe non-verbal clues:** Look around for non-verbal clues while getting briefed by the customer or observing how a task is performed. It may offer valuable latent needs for product development.

- **Response to competition on Products:** Observe and record how competitive products are used for Job-to-be-done. How are these products held, handled, installed, and operated?

- **Maintain the flow as per customer convenience:** Though as a researcher having an interviewing guideline, continue with the flow of the customer rather than the guide itself.

- **Focus on customer verbatim instead of narrating to early interpretation:** Audio or video recording of customer verbatim could offer immense benefits instead of writing what the researcher understood.

  Most importantly, shrug off the bias that, as a researcher, "I know everything that the market needs" syndrome.

Interpreting Customer Need Data

Information received during the interview, focus group moderations, or on-site real-use experiences; Data collected is processed in a simplistic way to translate into customer requirements -

- Converting all the notes, audio, and video inferences into written notes and statements

- Contents or interview notes are analyzed by team members; each team member may pick up varied unique interpretations. Hence it is recommended that

the statement interpretation be made by more than one team member. The contents are expressed as specifically as possible; the statement shall not contain what the product should not do but a positive toner about what is expected. The statements may also avoid using words like "should" and "must". It shall focus on what the customer expected the product to be doing, not the solution in mind.

- Write down all statements on a card or workbook, or sticky notes

- Cluster the statement in a group based on similarity and eliminate redundant statements.

- Enhance nested level up by grouping similar clusters to have a maximum of 5-6 groups and label each group appropriately.

2. **Quantification of the relative importance of data:**

   i. Generally, hierarchy is also done within each group for primary and secondary needs. Each of the latent needs is marked specifically as a MUST to highlight for consideration during the product concept stage.

   ii. Attach relative importance to each of the needs for ease of addressing and prioritizing

   iii. Typically, relative importance identifications are made to set prioritization, resource allocation etc. Prioritization inputs may be arrived at with a discussion with the team participating in interviews or also by interviewing a set of

customers again who were interviewed or through a questionnaire separately with reference statements. Remember not to have too many statements in a questionnaire to motivate enough respondents to participate, e.g., questions not to be in 100s.

3. **Reflection on process and outcome:** Having completed the cycle of customer identification, it is good to reflect on the following:

   i. Are the results and customer requirements in-line with anticipation?

   ii. Did we cover all target customer segments and geographies?

   iii. Are there any completely tangential elements or great surprises in the requirement documents

   iv. Do we see a clear alignment with the product development team on customer requirements?

   v. Do we need to revisit a certain set of customers for reevaluation and further clarifications?

   vi. Are there a set of customers who are a part of an ongoing engagement for product concept development processes?

   vii. Are we able to see longer tenure beyond today's needs and technologies on hand? Are there any weak signals (futuristic demands) left out of innovation needs that would enlighten future days of product usage?

    viii. Are there any further process improvements needed to make the process efficient and sufficient to work on product concepts on current project mission or future cases?

4. Potential customer revisits: Having completed customer needs identification; there are good possibilities and opportunities to revisit selected customers in the following contexts.

    i. Interesting set of customers offered insights in contrast to the envisaged product and solutions

    ii. Customers who would like to be a part of the concept development cycle.

    iii. Customers in favour of collaboration and also "co-creation."

    iv. Potential customers for prototype testing

    v. Group of customers where requirements offered are inconsistent with the collective knowledge of the development team and mainstream customers.

    vi. Non-customers but have the potential to contribute

Exercises

1. List a set of metrics about the infrastructure needed to promote two-wheelers in your market powered by Electricity

2. List a set of metrics about the passenger shelter on a busy road to support passengers awaiting public transport. Consider a life span of a minimum of 10x years for the proposed shelter.

Summary

In organizations, for any new product, process, or system to be initiated, there are a host of factors that are taken into consideration and studied in-depth before getting consent. This chapter is about the Product Development Process and the steps which are followed from scratch. Prior to any product approval, there is the planning stage. This involves weighing the overall pros and cons, which are:- the most suitable market segment and opportunity, evaluating the latest technology, the actual manufacturing process, and the organization's goals, vision, and mission.

Also, the external economic environment, risks, and assumptions are important considerations. Of course, the customer is always the King, so their needs and demands form an essential component of the product development process. Hence, customers and ways to know about their requirements are at the fulcrum of this chapter on Design Thinking.

Nowadays, there are umpteen methods for customer need identification. As per studies by top companies like McKinsey have revealed that customers desire innovation, though companies have not scaled up enough on this. Apart from the general, primary and secondary needs, organizations should also address the 'latent needs' of consumers that may have been overlooked till now. The reason being that these latent needs are not easily expressed, but it is the expertise of the creative team to extract them by minute observation.

To wrap up; Customer requirement gathering with a systematic approach of direct interactions, moderation and deep immersion around the real-use environment offers significant insights into product concept development. This process clearly addresses the customer's "job-to-be-done", leading to customer delight.

Chapter III

The Art of Applying Creativity & Idea Generation to Create Affordable yet WOW Solutions

Creativity, Idea generation, or concept development are key steps in the product development phase, as well as in addressing design problems or even other business issues. In the previous chapter on customer opportunity and need identification, we understood processes and also the critical dependency of a quality statement of customer needs that supports their "Job-to-be-done". This also covers elements like addressing latent needs which are difficult to express or that are easily uncovered during customer conversations.

Customer needs collected and presented among the product team is not technical specification but needs to be translated into form, function and target specifications, etc. Normally target specifications, which are approximate at this stage, are set. However, a particular technology is not chosen until enough ideas or solution concepts are generated, and then the most suitable one is selected. The specification sheet contains detailed parameters, ideal measurements for various parameters, and a minimal agreeable specification that makes products commercially viable too.

Following the finalization of a set of technical specifications, we engage in creative exploration to generate additional ideas. Although the following steps are recommended for the technology sector, they can also be adapted for non-technical domains too to address business challenges likewise.

"Having a not-so-great idea but poor implementation may still have a chance of some success. However, no matter how efficient the execution, a bad idea will fail.

Idea generation and solution concept steps: Creativity is an important element to kick-start any invention and innovation that leads to new products, product enhancements, services, solutions, and business concepts. In Part-I, we learned in detail about creativity applicable to business areas.

In this section, we touch upon how a problem or challenge is addressed, leading to innovative solutions.

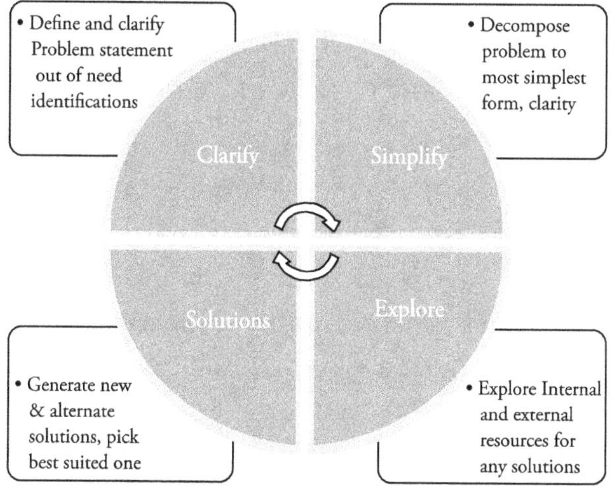

1. **Problem Statement and Clarification:** This step enables understanding of challenges and alignment of customer need statements and mission statements related to the project. This also ensures compatibility with the first set of specifications proposed by the product development teams.

   Recall the famous mission statement of President John F Kennedy; *"I believe that this nation should commit itself to achieving the goal, before this decade is out, of landing a man on the moon and returning him safely to earth"*. This statement has clarity on goals, challenges and timelines.

2. **Breakdown into smaller chunks:** Consider launching a new fabric washing machine for a developing market. While we begin with a designer approach, start decomposing tasks like Type (Hardness) of water being used, Types of fabric to be washed, capacity and drum drive, motor type, kind of power supplies it operates, operator interface, fabric loading, Inlet and drainage mechanism, safety functions, and so on.

   This step is also known as decomposing; problems are broken down into a series of simple and easy tasks to the extent that these tasks are easily understandable; they can be tracked, measured, and analyzed to be solved and combined further as a system. This approach simplifies the process of addressing complex challenges too.

3. **Explore external and internal sources:** With the decomposition of the problem into smaller ones, we start exploring solutions from both external to the organization and also within.

    An external search is about navigating through potential solutions with existing technology in the market, patents search for relevance, licensing, etc. Benchmarking through market exploration, competition play, and expert consultations are sources for solutions. Benchmarking of competitive products offers potential solutions for current problems and also about the strengths and weaknesses of the competition. The most important source may also be some of the customers, lead users, extreme users, or customers opting for co-creation.

    The advantage of decomposing and external search is that solutions available in a certain segment may also be potentially adapted to new situations on hand, though they belong to a completely different set of fields. Recall that composites developed in the defence sector were adapted in the development of low-weight solutions for polio-affected children to reduce fixture weights.

    An external search is a continuous process during the product development process. Relatively, much focus on adapting existing solutions in a variety of ways makes it efficient so that the most concerning problems where solutions don't exist may be focused more intensely and develop solutions that are new.

Internal search includes brainstorming or SCAMPER {Substitute, **C**ombine, **A**dapt, **M**odify (**M**agnify or **m**inimize), **P**ut to other use, **E**liminate, **R**everse/ Rearrange} methods for idea generation and selection. An internal search may include individual and group consultations.

4. **Generating new ideas:** Creativity and innovation activities within the organization offer the most effective solutions for critical problems on-hand. One of the effective methods is to use the brainstorming method for idea generation. This process was conceptualized and developed by Osborn in the 1940s and leverages largely on creativity and ideas emanating from experiences and knowledge within the team. In this process, solutions are created by effectively bringing out and adapting solution creations.

Thomas Edison, a prolific inventor, believed that to discover a good idea, one must generate many ideas. Quality emerges from quantity. He set idea quotas for all his workers, and his own quota was one minor invention every 10 days and a major invention every six months. What it means is the first idea may not always be the best idea, and it is necessary to generate more and more ideas in order to select the best one out of many.

With this open-minded approach, a large number of ideas are triggered, deliberated among a group of people, and gradually moved in the direction of quality ideas, filtering and aligning them for the best solutions.

Following are some of the basic guidelines to realize the best results out of brainstorming sessions:

- **Deferred Judgments:** Very basic foundation of brainstorming is to generate as many ideas from the team by way of recognizing and motivating participants to bring out innovative ideas. Even If any idea from a team member is not great, the best practice is to defer judgments about the idea. Instead, reframe how this idea can further be improvised. This enables participants to be open and contribute ideas. As a ground rule of creativity, a premise is to shred being judgmental about oneself and others.

- **Motivate to generate a lot of ideas:** The greater the number of ideas generated, the more likely the chance of a better solution fit with extensive exploration happening over there. Initially, focusing on quantity opens the door for ideas that may appear to be poor but may come to the fore. Each idea can inspire others to build over another's idea to produce seemingly better solutions.

- **Divergent technique:** Encourage the team to think out of the world, wild ideas that may result in seemingly impossible solutions. This opens up space for exploring solutions that were not thought of at some stage previously. This also encourages a greater number of ideas to build upon further.

- **Leverage sketches and storyboards:** When proposing or demonstrating potential solutions, expressions through texts and verbatim may not be efficient. Depicting the solutions by way of two-dimensional sketches makes it easy to express and understand. The focus here is not on the quality of sketches, but Concepts expressed, making product development successful.

  Ensure the availability of abundant sketching materials like color pencils, paper, and sketching aids.

  Sketches have an advantage for innovative solutions and storytelling. And will be Provocative, exploratory, trigger questions, suggestive, propose something, stimulate new ideas, also tentative in nature, and a storytelling tool.

A sample image kit will be useful in relating to solution development

Use of 3D sketch models

Solution concepts are expressed by using 3D models created using foams, thermocol, cardboard, clay, 3D printing, paper models, rubber, wood, nails, scissors, tape, glue, etc. When a thorough understanding of a specific problem and its solution is required, three-dimensional models that present form, shape and spatial representation come in handy. Occasionally, even a physical interface for the user is also presented (like a lever, knobs, etc.)

3D modelling offers a detailed look and feel, also represented well when someone is not good at sketching methods. This method also helps in quick prototyping to solicit customer feedback.

For example, a 3D cardboard model of a new washing machine to get a three-dimensional look, feel, interfaces, and spatial representation. This cardboard is also shaped, cut, and glued to represent a door, washing solution slots, operator interface area, water inlet and outlet, and other components.

Explore systematically

Once multiple ideas or solutions for each decomposed problem are explored thoroughly, the most suitable idea is selected to work further. These selected ideas are reviewed, manipulated, modified, and readjusted in various combinations to arrive at a combined system solution. A solution combination technique is useful for detailed exploration, and the best solutions are arrived at and selected.

How to pick the final solution

Open Multi-voting, Secret ballot, scoring matrix, Benefit vs effort listing, Group consensus, Leader's decisions, market testing, and online community ratings. Usually, multi-voting or secret voting methods are used when decisions need to be made quickly.

Before we pick the final, make it a point to ponder about the exploration of complete solution space, functional diagrams are looked into for alternatives, external search and resources are explored thoroughly, and every idea is accepted for exploration, and debated in detail.

Prototyping

With the selection of a solution, prototypes are created to communicate about the product, learn about it, and integrate with further elements as a system and as a milestone in product development. Prototypes are used for getting to know how a product looks and feels in case of physical product target functioning.

Prototypes may be physical versions or Analytical ones depending on the development cycle and criticality of the specification being tested for.

Within the dimension of the physical prototype, further options are to check for-

a. "*Comprehensive*" which focuses on every element of the product and is near to use and type.

b. "Focus type" prototypes to implement one or other attributes of the product instead of the full-fledged product. Focus-type prototypes include models made out of foam to explore.

A separate set of Analytical prototypes too are created for the Comprehensive or Focus type; For example, the Comprehensive type by dynamic simulations (not feasible in all cases) and focused simulations like testing the steering system or simulation model for a motor or a brake system in Automotive.

Comprehensive prototypes have their own challenges like, time involved, and investments needed apart from technical and market risks.

Summary

The previous chapter concentrated on customer needs and how they are gathered. This chapter discusses the next stage and how to proceed after collecting customer needs. These are still in the process of being organized into a specific form, function, and target specification. Technical specifications are not finalized yet until more ideas are generated. Thereafter, the most appropriate one is chosen. Idea generation is a continuous process; even after technical specifications have been established, more ideas are encouraged.

What steps are followed to address the problem has been elaborated on in this chapter-

a. Define and clarify the problem out of need identification

b. Simplify the problem to make it easily comprehensible

c. Generate new & alternate solutions; choose the best

d. Explore internal and external resources for solutions

   Some of the best ways to have a collection of ideas are-

   - Brainstorming is an effective and time-tested method for generating new ideas. Once there is a stack of ideas, it is simple to filter through them and select the best.

   - Motivate people to come up with novel solutions, divergent thinking, and outlandish ideas. Allow

for the free flow of ideas by deferring judgment. 3D modelling, sketching, and other similar tools are excellent aids to help in the process.

- The final step is to go through the prototyping step to get to know the look and feel of physical products in either physical form or analytical reviews.

Chapter-IV

Design Thinking for Services – The New Way of Delighting Customers

In Chapter- III, we had an opportunity to learn more about product development processes, such as opportunity identification, capturing customer needs, Idea generation and solution offering as we progressed towards concept development steps. As a product, we recognized the benefit and need for breaking problems or decomposing them to their simplest form in order to create a solution.

Since our technology industry and non-technology sector span beyond just products, it is beneficial to extend our Design Thinking approach to service areas. Specifically, India and other emerging markets are highly dependent on the service industry, offering an excellent customer experience that would yield great business results.

In this chapter, we shall be looking at how various customer touch points may be enhanced for better customer experiences with innovative ideas while also raising the living standards of the general population.

To start with, let's have common definitions and understanding of Product, Services, and Product-services system bundling.

Product

Represented by physical goods delivered to the customer, normally produced at one location and consumed at another. Producers may have limited access to end user points, likely with final customers likely served through multi-channel supply chains. The producer is highly unlikely to be at the customer's place during consumption. Customers enjoy benefits out of materialistic properties, form, spatial properties and how well the product matches the intended use. For example When Bosch Rexroth Company, primarily an engineering goods manufacturer, provides hydraulic control components, pumps, and industrial automation products such as programmable controllers, drives, and motors. These products are finally owned by customers and delivered through projects or OEM-supplied machinery.

Services

Services are characterized by intangible products, with production and consumption occurring together or simultaneously. The service provider is highly expected to be engaged throughout the customer journey and be connected with the producer or service provider. For example, A health insurance service provider offers protection to individuals or groups with financial protection against losses or cost of recovery inflicted by a set of medical challenges. Here the service is intangible financial services to reduce the financial burden by partially or completely covering the cost of health care.

Product-Services Bundling

Rail transportation services had trains as a product and services covering the whole gamut of the train reservation system, check-out, refund, booking, pantry services, upholstery services for berths during overnight travel and so on. Other examples of such bundling are automotive rental services, hospital or health care services, restaurants serving food, and photocopier cum printer rentals.

Similar to the product development concept shared wherein Opportunity identification, and customer needs identifications are embedded well to finally create innovative products, service designs are also addressed in the same way.

In this chapter, we shall focus on just service design concepts and understand Design Thinking approach for customer delight.

Services characteristics

Like products, services also have similarities in the product development process, such as understanding customer needs, having a certain structure, and testing. However, some of the elements of services are prominently distinguishable in certain areas, for e.g., customer presence during service delivery, multiple customer interfaces or touch points, and interactive and iterative transactions, with each touch point providing innovative experiences with variety and a dynamic environment.

Time to respond, resolution and total turnaround time, waiting times etc., carry criticality to customer success factors. Invariably, any sluggish or delayed response causes huge customer dissatisfaction, e.g., a slow internet causing a poor touch point experience, which may cause a customer to abandon a buy at the final checkout for a shopping cart. Such experiences may be addressed by having the sufficient and right capacity, and infrastructure established considering the present and anticipated market demands.

Some of the services may be less frequently used, and some may be more repetitive. The modular structure of service offerings provides significant advantages in serving customers in terms of ease of deployment, scalability, and management. (e.g., ERP software is the best example where the customer has a choice to pick certain modules prominently).

Enhancement of services

A product, as we have seen and experienced, is represented by tangible goods in physical form, a set of geometry, and spatial presence. However, since services are intangible to a very large extent, they are better explained through texts and storyboards, extensive interfaces or touch points that follow a sequence of actions between the service provider and customer. The quality and efficacy of these various touch points (or sequences) form an integral part of customer satisfaction and offer enormous opportunities for innovating and improving customer experiences. In other words, service sequences are also decomposed to depict customer needs in detail, allowing opportunities for improvements and innovations.

Customer Journey Mapping: Typical services experience cycle starts with a customer's desire to shop or buy a service, purchase or shop either at a physical store or on-portal, consume the services, reflect on the experience and repeat with another set of desired services.

The above experience cycle can be further detailed or decomposed by a set of customer touch points where different processes happen in the foreground, a varied set of supporting actions happen in the background and services are delivered on the journey. This is also called customer experience mapping. Once detailed customer experience mapping is done, each touch point is evaluated for further innovation possibilities to enhance customer experiences. Customer experience journey mapping is also known as Customer empathy journey, capturing the physical and emotional experiences of customers while availing services or interfacing with various touch points.

A deeper understanding of the customer experience journey helps in the delivery of a differentiated customer experience. Customer experience journey mapping assists in knowing those critical turning points in customer relationships that can make or break. Such mappings are also carried out based on existing customer feedback, employee feedback or customer immersion journeys (undercover journeys at the frontline).

Consider an example of a service experience while purchasing Senior citizens' day care services and map various touch points, and review opportunities for enhancing customer experiences.

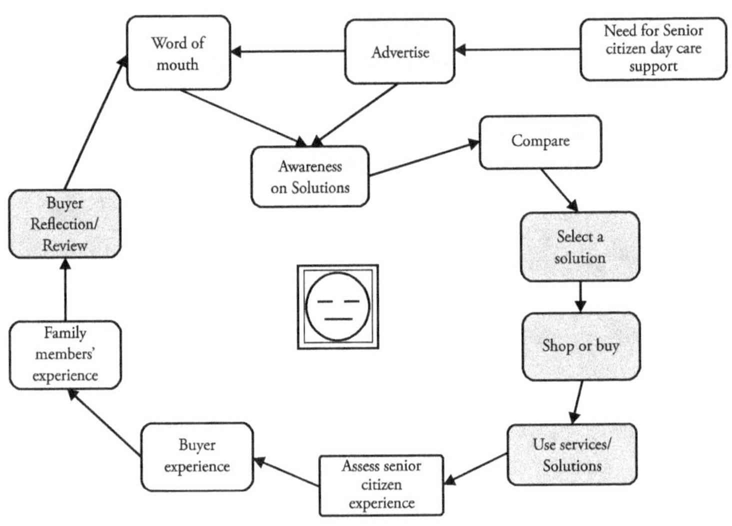

The journey begins with a need for service experience in the form of daycare support for a senior citizen. There is already some awareness of the availability of such services through word-of-mouth or advertisements. The buyer compares different solutions for these needs and selects a particular one. Further, after buying, the customer utilizes those daycare services and may be assessed for the outcome and experience of these services. The next step is to look for the buyer's experience (where the buyer is not the ultimate service user), as well as reflections from family members around the user. The Final step is to assess and review all experiences.

In this example, we can notice that the boxes or touch points highlighted are potential opportunities for enhancing customer experiences by improving or offering better or more innovative offerings.

At each of the identified innovation opportunities, background influencers and front-end providers need to work closely in designing delightful customer experiences and deploying them for prototyping and expanded utilization.

Such a process will help in enhancing customer experiences, winning new or converting non-customers into customers, resulting in a successful service offering.

The customer empathy journey may also be mapped in a four-sector circle, each quartile representing what the customer "THINK", "SAYS", "FEELS", and DOES" to understand various emotional experiences and activities. Each of these sectors and its elements of experiences may be attached with an expressive symbol like emojis (☺) or (☹) or (😐)

The empathy journey may also be mapped by a linear, continuous flow diagram and interconnections, marked with experience symbols or texts for each touch point, to identify innovation opportunities instead of circular journey steps shared in the above example of senior citizen day care services.

These inputs from the empathy journey support creating greater UX (User experiences) for customers.

Further actions

Consider an example of buying online insurance, capture your experience journey and identify at least 3x areas or touch points for innovation opportunities.

Summary

We've seen design thinking in relation to the product development process so far; in this part, we see how the same principle applies to the services sector.

After all, it is not just products that we use; services are equally important. Though overall, the process is the same for both products and services, from opportunity identification to customer need identification. The main distinction is between physical goods and intangible products. Also, production and consumption occur concurrently, and there is customer empathy as an essential core.

Consumers and producers are involved for a longer time, requiring more interaction and empathy. For example, health insurance providers provide financial security to the beneficiary, implying a stronger bond. To improve customer services, a process known as customer experience journey mapping exists that paves the path for innovations. Aside from that, consistent customer feedback and evaluation results in happier customers. Several methods of mapping this customer empathy journey to get the best output have been highlighted here.

Chapter V

Commercializing Your Idea – Testing and Scaling the Product or Services

In the previous chapter, we discussed extending product design concepts to service design. Customer empathy journey mapping helps in understanding opportunities for innovation leading to customer delight. When we have both product and service concepts for an innovation ready, at some point, we start evaluating commercial viability.

Generally, there will be Go or NO-Go gates at various stages of the project development cycle, from project conceptualization to product development. This is to restate that commercialization, or financial viability, is not done only at the end of the product launch process.

By definition, the term commercialization refers to the transformation of ideas, knowledge, and innovation into greater wealth for individuals, organizations or societies at large. Commercialization is driven by market, profitability, and value creation for stakeholders with a positive return on investments. Investments may range into varied activities like R&D, licensing, capital goods like machinery, marketing, and niche creation.

In the context of the Design Thinking approach step, we shall consider some typical economic parameters like NPV, Cash flow, and Return on Investments (ROI) though there are many other elements such as Net working capital (NWC) and so on. Return on Investment rates are also connected with the prevailing economic situation, market and risks involved. Generally, the higher the risk, the higher the expected returns.

Furthermore, there would be other parameters that drive innovation adoption beyond the economics of the originator, which we shall dwell upon soon.

Net Present value (NPV): Net present value is the difference between the present value of cash inflow and the present value of cash outflows. NPV applies to a series of cash flows happening over different times. The net present value of a cash flow depends on discount rates (interest), the interval of time between now and cash flow. NPV is used widely in capital budgeting to assess and establish which projects are likely to turn great profits over a given time. NPV >0 is considered a positive indicator to go ahead with the project, NPV=0 means no significant loss or profit, and a negative NPV is generally a no-go for a project.

Z1= cash flow in time1 $\dfrac{z_1}{1+r}+\dfrac{z_2}{(1+r)^2}-X_0$

Z2= cash flow in time2

r= discount rate

X_0= cash outflow at time 0 (initial purchase price or initial investments)

Cash flows are discounted for two main reasons, (a) To account for the risk on investment, the higher the risk, the higher the discount rate and (b) To account for the time-value of money (To factor for inflation, interest rates, opportunity costs.

Though the NPV method is widely used, it has some of the following key challenges for analysis:

- List of assumptions and the level of impact if an assumption is incorrect.

- Sensitivity to small changes in key assumptions and drivers

- May not reflect or consider impacts on an adjacent business or other related areas

- Does marketing spending truly reflect on sales results?

- A standard discount rate across a period of cash flow

- Cost of recycling or revenue of recycling factored rightly?

- Ramp-up cost and timing variability

- Susceptible to easy manipulations and driving results in biased ways

- Assumptions may go awfully wrong

Sensitivity Analysis

For a project, an economical result like NPV depends on many independent variables that impact either mildly or severely. A sensitivity analysis is done to assess the extent of the impact of the variability. It is measured as a ratio of the Percent of change in output to the percentage extent of change in inputs. A high ratio indicates higher-sensitivity. This analysis is used to predict the outcome under certain conditions and considers appropriate measures to contain the outcomes affecting business negatively.

Sensitivity analysis also reveals whether I can continue to sell certain products at a loss while generating a stream of ongoing consumables and services revenue. Such an analysis also enables us to evaluate the potential entry of a new competitor or existing competitor responses.

To learn more about NPV, consider a live example of a project decision cycle for "Go" or "No-Go", then do a sensitivity analysis to see changes or the extent of changes in NPV.

Negative NPV project pursuits

While a positive NPV would signal a clear go-ahead with project or decision stages, a negative NPV usually results in a No-Go. However, negative NPV projects or products out of innovation are still pursued under the following circumstances-

- As a "spending" instead of an "investment" to build competencies for the future.

- As development of goodwill with society at large

- Development of product as early testing

- May bring impact on other sets of adjacent businesses positively

- Need to play by virtue of market position to remain in the competition, expecting a future change in market dynamics.

- Using as technology transfer to leverage innovation and make technology available to promote industry-wide economic growth or offer environmental and social benefits to larger society than just being commercial (direct benefit), E.g., In the health care and education sector, addressing environmental concerns etc.

Summary

When product or service concepts are ready for innovation, we move on to the next and most important stage: assessing commercial viability. Commercialization means delving into the wealth aspect of innovation or wealth creation.

To accomplish this, a number of economic factors, such as Net Present Value (NPV), Return on Investment (ROI), cash flow, and the overall economic environment, must be considered and studied.

The primary criterion for determining commercial viability is NPV, which is the difference between the present value of cash inflow and cash outflow. If this value is zero or negative,

the chances of earning money are slim. However, this method is not always 100% accurate because it is based on assumptions that are sometimes incorrect.

That is why a sensitivity analysis is performed: to avoid/ minimize any negative economic impact. In exceptional cases, innovative projects are pursued even if the NPV value is negative. Reasons include investing in future competencies, building goodwill with society, and developing products for early testing.

Chapter VI

Beware of Environmental Damages – Design For Environment

Design for Environment (DfE)

As the reader enters this chapter, so far confident that he or she has understood various steps of addressing opportunities, identifying customer needs, and developing a potential solution, the final lap is important as a responsible Designer.

As we approach the final leg of our understanding of the Design Thinking approach, it is essential to understand our responsibilities as great designers in terms of environmental aspects. Innovators' commitment to protecting our planet earth while we deliver innovative products and solutions goes a long way in benefiting society as a whole.

This image says a thousand words…! The above image set is self-explanatory from multiple perspectives.

Concerns about environmental impact, global warming, and scarcity of resources have grown in recent years. Humans continue to deplete the earth's resources and refill them back with toxic, solid wastes, which may take weeks, months, years and hundreds of years to disintegrate and be absorbed into the soil. Also, there has been an increase in the pollution of oceans and other water bodies. Air pollution is causing serious health concerns for humans and other forms of life on earth.

Design for Environment (DfE) or Green Design, in other words, adopts a broad concept of designing products and services to consume less energy and cleaner energy. The design approach puts efforts into the reduction of global warming primarily out of the burning of fossil fuels. However, the challenges of obtaining material on a recurring basis remain, which are being addressed during the design process.

DfE is a method used to minimize or completely eliminate the environmental impacts of a product over its life cycle, extending all the way to disposal and recycling. The target is also to reduce costs or maintain while delivering better quality products.

DfE Process: Following are brief steps followed to address environmental challenges, and the key pivotal factor is the quality of decisions made at various decision points on DfE.

With the right integration of the DfE process in product development, significant results can be achieved in Green Design.

1. **Mission Statement:** While defining a project or framing a related mission statement, a company decision on Green Design may be specified as overall goals (E.g., There shall be zero emission of hazardous gases, Carbon Neutrality, or Zero Landfill as goals)

2. **Product Concept and system level stage:** DfE and Material guidelines to ensure Material targeted to be part of the concept aligns with the Mission statement.

3. **Detailed Engineering:** Asses in detail about environmental impacts of targeted material, and alternatives and refine design engineering further to ensure the lowest possible environmental impact on a sustained basis

4. **Serial production or ramp-up stage:** On-going improvements of processes on Green Design and potential level-up targets. This stage is also an opportunity to review results and reflect on DfE processes.

Product Life cycle Assessment: (LCA)

The Life-Cycle Assessment step evaluates the quantitative impact on the environment of a product over its entire life cycle, including disassembly and recycling or reuse.

This process may call for the use of special tools or software and expertise to make a detailed analysis.

The steps involved in the LCA cycle are-

- Alignment of the overall goal of the enterprise to contain environmental impact and strategic goals.

- Identify all materials involved in each of the life cycle stages of the product, including disposal or recycling.

- Determination and tagging of energy sources used for each material.

- Identification of outputs at each stage and wastages and waste recoveries involved.

- Quantification of material, energy, and waste.

- Making appropriate DfE decisions based on the above and the consideration of costs

General guidelines at each stage of LCA for DfE

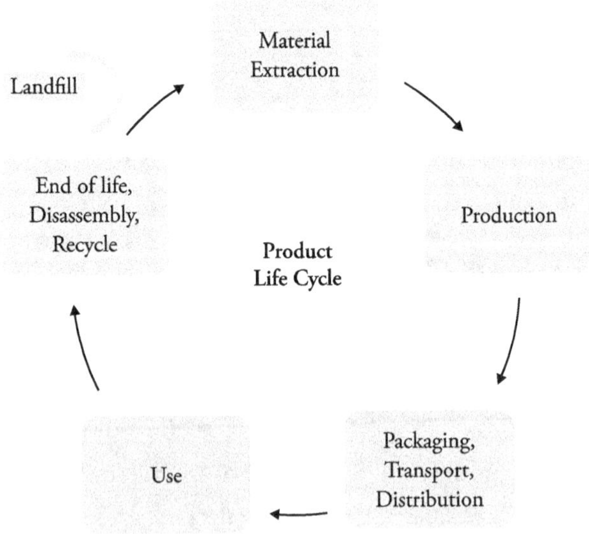

Material Extraction

- Avoid or reduce the use of toxic, hazardous, or any other potentially polluting materials that are unfriendly to the environment.

- Minimize the use of materials.

- Use material which is natural, renewable, or recycled.

- Design optimization to reduce overall material usage.

- Capture and reuse all hazardous material, if any.

- Minimize the variety of materials used.

Production

- Minimize energy-intensive processes

- Keep the optimal design of capacities

- Reduce the extent of design safety factors being stacked-up

- Capture all toxic gas and waste generated from entering the environment, adopting modern technologies

- Avoid or reduce downtimes and rework

Packaging, Transport & Distribution

- Use of environmentally friendly packing materials, reusable contents

- Reuse of container or packaging materials, enhance the reliability of such packing materials

- Use optimal routing and energy-efficient transport system (avoiding airborne transport of heavy goods)

- Optimizing sourcing and production facilities, being closer to a large cluster of customs or users

Use

- Use of products or plants to their designed capacity where possible to get the highest desired efficiency levels

- Run on non-fossil fuels, recover energy out of wastes (Recovery processes)

- Running in Default OFF mode when not in use, avoid idle running of rotating equipment, heating, cooling systems, sufficient insulations at cooling, heating systems

- Use energy-efficient appliances across utilities and production systems

- The target for reduction of WAGES (Water, Air, Gas, Energy, Steam) consumed on a continual basis (Plan for same at Design stages)

End of Life, Disassembly, recycle

- Do not combine incompatible materials during recycling

- Do not fasten permanently or enable ease of separation of recycling different classes of materials (E.g., threaded metal inserts into plastic)

- Label materials for recycling

- Use no surface treatments and avoid painting materials

- Stimulate possible refurbishing/remanufacturing

A decision point for determining whether a product is environmentally friendly from the point of disassembly is that we are able to take it apart easily with standard tools.

The BMW car Z1 is an early example of the incorporation of the Disassembly concept. Plastic exteriors can be removed from metal chassis in 20 minutes. The doors, front and rear side panels, and bumpers have been manufactured with recycled plastics. These items are fastened with push-in/out methods instead of screws and glues at most places.

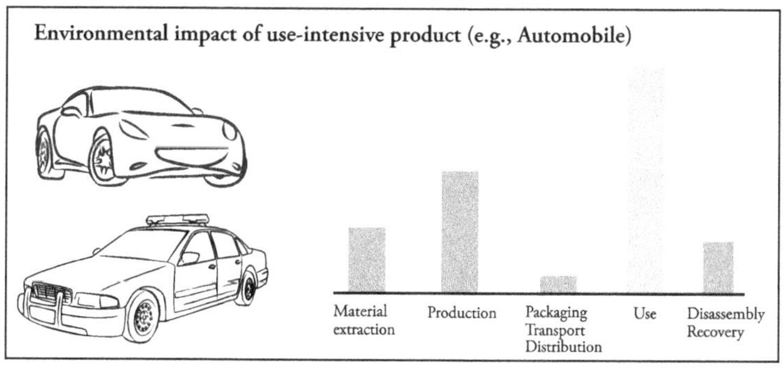

Environmental, Social & Governance (ESG) Initiative

Design for the environment or green design approach of Design Thinking resonates well with the ESG (Environmental, Social & Governance) initiatives being pursued globally, specifically in the tech sector. DfE can be used as an important lever in compliance with ESG.

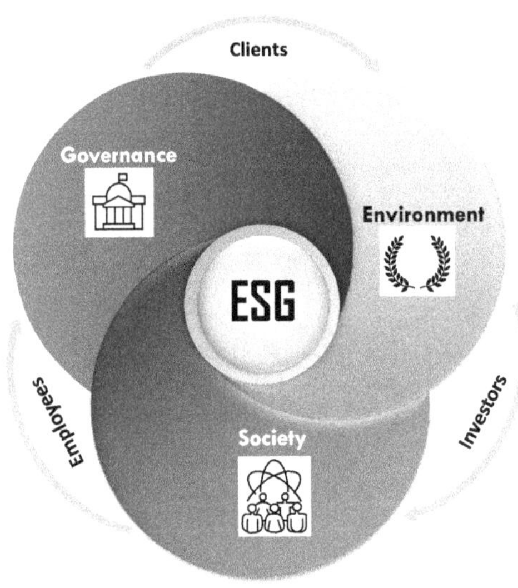

What is ESG, and why is it important for enterprises?

Since the last few years, sustainable business models, climate change, and ESG reportings have been at the forefront as global economies race towards achieving "Net-zero" or "Carbon Neutrality" by 2050. Even though the term ESG is used in the context of investing, clients of technology companies are becoming more and more alert about the ESG performance of their vendors, and partners, extending to employees.

Investors are increasingly keenly discussing the environmental and societal impact of corporates beyond shareholder value, considering ESG as one of the key elements of investment strategy.

Millennials are keenly watching and interested in being a part of sustainable organizations, having a purpose and commitment to ESG. Employees have always been important stakeholders influencing the strategy, and ESG principles have become a huge competitive advantage in attracting and retaining talents.

ESG is a framework that helps stakeholders to understand how an organization is performing around sustainability and managing risks and opportunities.

ESG has evolved from concerns about health, safety, pollution control, and corporate social responsibilities.

While we can focus on a specific topic of the Environment aspect; the following key elements reinforce ESG compliances from an organization and Design for the environment focusing on LCA (Life Cycle Assessment) concepts to create a win-win situation-

- Climate change and carbon footprint
- Green technology and innovation for clients
- Water and waste management

Design thinking participants have immense opportunities to contribute towards the ESG journey, enabling organizations to have a strong competitive advantage.

Summary

In the past, manufacturing firms were concerned with meeting regulations connected with just manufacturing processes on pollution control and energy consumption. However, new regulations are bringing more focus to the product as a whole, considering material content and its environmental impact over the life cycle. A genuine environment-friendly product is one that has neutrality on environmental impact and also reduces current levels of adverse environmental impacts; It also extends its value by converting a product into an input for the next stage instead of creating waste at the end of the life cycle.

Conclusion

Ready to be Creative
and START your Reinvention journey

Now, a well narrated book on Creativity, Reinvention and its grand contours is completed with set of tools, in your hands. Some of you would realize few approaches and tools are already known in one or other formats, and few are new to imbibe in work life and personal life. Hope, you are able to pick some baby steps in assessing your abundance of creativity in realizing your hoped for future. You have created the beautiful life and profession that made what you are, and you can create a new one and unstuck from where you are for better, focus on path of possibilities.

While we strongly reassure ourselves that we cannot predict the future, but we have or can build the capabilities and action to create the future. Reinvention approach supports assessing scenario, grasping and interpreting weak signals leading to a clear anticipation of change. Timely intervention and designing, implementing a change to sustain progress and grow further on the lines of making competition irrelevant is the need. Instill a system that enables and sustains reinvention on on-going basis like a frequent shower. Whether it is an incremental change or a radical one in the midst of Calm

Ocean or huge disruptions, at least some move can make for your way forward to survive and thrive for success.

Unable to relinquishing arrogance of past success, "too big to fail" attitude, resting on laurels of pass success are clear obstacles for growth and survival. Creating future organization within the current set-up while enhancing performance efficiency of current with dual organization approach, leadership can ensure continued growth. While experimenting innovating products and business models with new, one may tend to fail; success stays in learning from failures and at cheap, because you are resilient and failure tolerant.

Business environment, technology, competition, customer demands and demographics keep changing at a much faster pace which we are experiencing and in near future too.

The numbers of enterprises listed among as Fortune-500 are no longer same fortunate enough to be in list when compared over decades. Life expectancy of organizations those not reinventing one are shortening and you will ensure, surely yours' is not the one among.

Reinvention is always a work-in-progress and cycle repeats frequently.

There is enough knowledge around the environment to be learnt by way of Biomimicry, let us commit ourselves to save and live in harmony with nature around.

I am hopeful, this book is helping you crafting your professional journey in reaching your goals, reaching destination of hoped future. Am sure you will enjoy the journey too, making you much happier and confident than ever before.

Bibliography

A.G. Lafley and Roger L Martin, (2013, PLAYING TO WIN- HOW REALLY STRATEGY WORKS, Boston: Harvard Business Review Press

Bill Burnett and Dave Evans, (2018), Designing your life, London: Penguin Random House

Clayton M. Christensen, Taddy Hall, Karen Dillon, David S Duncan, (2016), Competing against Luck, New York: HarperCollins Publishers

David B Yoffie, Michael A Cusumano, (2015), Strategy Rules, Five Timeless Lessons from Bill Gates, Andy Grove, and Steve Jobs, New York: HarperCollins Publishers

Drew Boyd and Jacob Goldernberg, (2013), INSIDE THE BOX, A Proven System of Creativity for Breakthrough Results, New York: Simon & Schuster Paperbacks

Govindarajan V, (2016), The Three-Box Solution, Boston, HBR Press

Harvard Business Essentials - Managing Creativity and Innovation, Boston, Harvard Business School Publishing Corporation

Michael Ray and R Myers, (1986), Creativity in Business, New York: Doubleday & Co Inc.

Matthew S Olson and Derek Van Bever, (2008), STALL POINTS - Most Companies Stop Growing-Yours Doesn't Have To: Rave Media Publication

Nadya Zhexembayeva, (2020), How to Thrive in Chaos-The Chief Reinvention Officer Handbook: IDEAPRESS PUBLISHING

Steven Eppinger and Karl T Ulrich, (2000), Product Design and Development: Irwin/McGraw-Hill

Tim Brown, (2020), HBR's 10 MUST READS, Featuring Design Thinking, Boston, Harvard Business School Publishing Corporation

Kevin Coyne, Patricia Gorman Clifford, and Renée Dye, (December 2007), Breakthrough Thinking from Inside the Box- HBR Article

Tony McCaffrey and Jim Pearson, (December 2015), Find Innovation Where You Least Expect It, HBR Article:

Vijay Govindarajan and Chris Trimble, Building Breakthrough Businesses Within Established Organizations, HBR Article

Many anecdotes, examples and stories shared in the book are gathered over a period of time from various sources like Twitter, LinkedIn, other social media, periodicals, expert speakers, business meetings, conferences etc.,

Every effort has been made to give due credits for the sources of material contained herein. If I inadvertently omitted to credit someone, it shall be rectified during further publications if brought to my attention.

Other Sources

https://hbr.org/2006/02/
the-why-what-and-how-of-management-innovation

https://hbr.org/2002/08/creativity-is-not-enough

https://www.valuer.ai/
blog/50-examples-of-corporations-that-failed-to-innovate-and-
missed-their-chance

https://www.automation.com/en-us/articles/
november-2020/225-years-bosch-rexroth-high-tech-pioneer

https://www.boschrexroth.com/en/in/company/our-history/

www.ingramcontent.com/pod-product-compliance
Lightning Source LLC
LaVergne TN
LVHW041306200726
843509LV00009B/394